tales of Graceful Aging
from the
Planet Denial

Tales of Graceful Aging
from the
Planet Denial

Nicole Hollander

BROADWAY BOOKS
NEW YORK

PUBLISHED BY BROADWAY BOOKS

Published in the United States by Broadway Books, an imprint of The Doubleday
Broadway Publishing Group, a division of Random House, Inc., New York.
www.broadwaybooks.com

BROADWAY BOOKS and its logo, a letter B bisected on the diagonal, are trademarks
of Random House, Inc.

Book design by Diane Hobbing of Snap-Haus Graphics

Library of Congress Cataloging-in-Publication Data
Hollander, Nicole.
    Tales of graceful aging from the planet denial / Nicole Hollander. — 1st ed.
      p. cm.
    1. Aging—Humor.   I. Title.

    PN6231.A43H66 2007
    818'.5402—dc22

ISBN 978-0-7679-2653-9

PRINTED IN THE UNITED STATES OF AMERICA

10 9 8 7 6 5 4 3 2 1

First Edition

THIS BOOK IS FOR MY FRIENDS...

When other friendships have been forgot
Ours will still be hot...

—FROM "FRIENDSHIP,"
MUSIC AND LYRICS BY COLE PORTER

"Getting old in America ... best to do it somewhere else."

—*SYLVIA* CARTOON STRIP, 1990

Contents

Tales of Graceful Aging
from the
Planet Denial

Epiphanies

MY HEAD is SPLITTING! Is it A Migraine... OR - AN EPIPHANY?

Three girlfriends go to the movies

The two girlfriends and I are going to the movies. Someone who looks about twelve is selling the tickets. She looks at me and I prepare myself to be complimented on my earrings, scarf, lipstick . . . any number of things because I know I look adorable.

She says, "Will that be senior citizen, ma'am?" Behind me the girlfriends suck in their breath. They are happy they made me leave that cute little revolver that I bought in case some man proposed to me and wouldn't take no for an answer at home. They fear another traumatic event like the one when that kid tried to give me his seat on the bus. Big deal . . . He's young, his scars will heal.

But instead of reaching for the twelve-year-old in order to pull her through the small opening in the ticket window, I make a quick calculation. The number of movies I go to each month, multiplied by ten years and full price versus ten years of senior citizen discounted movies. I could probably buy a nice condo in the south of France with the money I'd save.

So I say in a shaky voice, "Yes, dearie, that'll be one senior citizen and two at regular price." The girlfriends speak as one: "Make that three, dearie."

Chapter 1

IF 60 is the new 40, when will I be 30?

60 is the new 40.

OKAY, SO SAY YOUR FAIRY GODMOTHER MAKES YOU 30 AGAIN? terrific, RIGHT? WHAT IF SHE HAS A DARK SENSE OF HUMOR, AND MAKES YOU sixteen AGAIN?

The sixties are your most creative years

I'm with the girlfriends. I am all abuzz with my news. I say, "The sixties are the most creative time in our lives. Women get a second wind in their sixties, they conquer new worlds, make change happen, reinvent themselves, make a contribution."

"Uh-huh," says Audrey. "Who told you that?" "It's everywhere," I say. "The sixties are the new forties. You can't pick up a magazine, a Sunday supplement, a book, without being told that this is your time. Now! Don't lie around like a slug. Make it happen."

"Well," says Audrey, struggling to get up from the couch, "I guess we better start. As I recall we are all in our mid-sixties and if we don't get busy, we will have missed the moment and will suddenly find ourselves in our seventies with nothing to show for it."

"I have some suggestions," I say shyly.

"Well, of course you do. It's too much to expect that in your sixties you would suddenly notice the need for silence and for contemplation, for being by yourself and leaving others alone to think their own thoughts," says Audrey.

"Please," I snarl. "I've spent too much time in silent meditation. I say it's time for action."

"That silent meditation," asks Audrey, "was that, like, for

five minutes sometime in 1976, during the Carter adminis-
tration?"

"Okay. I'm for making waves," says Bitsy. "Let's march for
peace, for getting out of Iraq . . . for an immigration plan that
is compassionate, for health insurance, just like the French."

"Oh, you mean, protesting for stuff like rescuing our
democracy," I say wistfully. "Civil liberties, all that ACLU
stuff. . . . Or fighting for education or public television, making the word *feminism* okay to say out loud again. And the
environment and global warming and cars that guzzle gas?"

"Yes," says Audrey. "I could get behind any one of those
things."

"Well forget it," I say. "That's not really the kind of thing I
had in mind. Let those in their thirties take up the mantle of
the big action, crowds of thousands, marching in the snow. I
will chug Baileys and hot chocolate while I watch them on
TV. I will criticize their signs, their organization, their choice
of celebrities, all from in front of the fire, while I crochet
baby clothes for imaginary grandchildren. That was not really
what I had in mind when I suggested that we contribute. I
was thinking of becoming litigious . . . in a small way. Or of
making a nuisance of ourselves in the cause of helping others by pointing out their shortcomings. Now is the time to
go to Trader Joe's and say, 'You have fabulous food on the
whole, your prices are fair, but your sushi is dry and unappe-
tizing and your cooked chicken and turkey, both bland disas-
ters.' This is the time to bring a class action suit against the
airports where men can get a shoe shine and women can't
have a manicure or a little touch-up on their roots to save
their lives."

8

"Wow," says Audrey. "You sure you can fit that into your tight schedule?"

"Yes," I say, ignoring the sarcasm. "I am sixty-seven, I have the time, and I have the energy. I can even interfere in friends' lives in a more consistently persistent way than I ever have before. I can stand, firm, combative, yet loving, and say: 'Audrey, get rid of that ugly couch before the termites carry it off and there are other colors besides white to paint a room.'" I look around. "Sally!" Sally has been looking out the window while I've been helping Audrey.

"Sally," I say, taking her face in my hands. "No more instant coffee. I can't take drinking brown water anymore. I will not stand for it. I want you to go out and buy an espresso machine, something that runs about three thousand dollars. It'll be worth it. You've got a few good years on your car yet, you don't need to buy a new Mini Cooper in ivory and black."

They are both in tears. I've done my work, time to watch my TiVoed *Gray's Anatomy*. Yes, I have TiVo and a satellite dish and I am certainly eyeing those phone/online/e-mail doohickeys to carry with me all the time, in case someone asks, "Do you know when the train for Lake Forest stops here and when it arrives in Lake Forest?" And I can quickly look it up on my BlackBerry-like thing.

Aftershock

The next day Sally calls with a question. "What happens when we are like ninety and no longer in our 'creative years' . . . ?" she whispers. "What happens when we are truly old?" I haven't the heart to tell her about assisted-living facilities. I tell her we will arrange to have her eaten by tigers.

Okay, what about assisted living, which are by all accounts dreary places filled with old people moving slowly about with walkers, looking for their next craft project?

I am sure that by the time I'm ready for assisted living, we will have a more enlightened attitude toward dying and Craigslist will offer heroin for barter or sale. A pal of mine said his mother lived with him the last year of her life and preferred Tylenol 3 to all else. He said, "Ma, you're blasted." She reminded him she was ninety.

Really, I should plan ahead; cultivate high school students, the ones with knowing looks, the scary-looking kids. Give them my business card; tell them to have their cells on all the time. I'll be in touch very soon with a business proposition.

Is there a woman among us who can tell a joke and remember the punch line?

I'm terribly excited. I tell the girlfriends that I have always wanted to tell a long convoluted joke that starts: A minister, a priest, and a rabbi walk into a bar . . . using a heavy Irish brogue. Although it seems to me that the funniest jokes often involve nuns and four-letter words. Even one of those jokes could be improved by performing it with an accent. In fact, one of the few jokes, really the only one, my husband ever told me, involved nuns in a cornfield with crows and an expletive. He has a Hungarian accent, which made it even better.

My mother and all her friends were incredibly witty. They could do twenty minutes off-the-cuff on a husband with a cold, but they didn't tell jokes. My mother could never remember a punch line and she was totally hopeless with accents, so the shaggy dog story about two leprechauns and the tiny nun, told with an Irish accent, was forever beyond her reach. "Girls," I say, "this does not have to be our destiny. We have two more decades than we thought to learn how to tell an ethnic joke."

I give them an assignment, which involves choosing secondhand joke books on eBay. I caution them against riddles, knock-knocks, and puns. I once spent a lovely afternoon at a bar on the beach in St. Pete. The blonde bartender knew a hundred blonde jokes, even phoned her boyfriend when she couldn't think of a punch line: "Why are blonde jokes one-liners? So men can understand them."

Pick a favorite joke. Mine would be one that involved lawyers. Here's a short one: What do you say about a lawyer buried up to the neck in sand? Not enough sand. But the one I want to find would start: A lawyer, a clergyman, and a gay kangaroo walk into a bar . . . The joke must take longer than four minutes to tell, must be one that demands that you force your audience to continue to listen even if their eyes glaze over, that you ignore their shifting in their seats and stay immune to their attempts to change the subject or to tell their own joke. This is best done when liquor is part of the scenario.

When you complete the first part of your assignment, we will bring in the voice coaches. Soon we will be ready for the ultimate test, taking our joke to the neighborhood bar, able to tell it with an Irish, Italian, Spanish, or Yiddish accent as the situation demands.

Wait! My new favorite joke is Why is a man better than a vibrator? Because a vibrator can't change a tire or replace a lightbulb. . . . Ask your guests to come up with a new punch line. This is a fun game to play at a bridal shower.

Finding your true vocation around forty, give or take a year

Now that I have the bonus of twenty or so years of renewed energy, I can start a new career. In fact, I must start a new career or be considered a slacker.

I've always wanted to be a detective. Oddly enough, I never wanted to be Nancy Drew. No, never Nancy Drew. She seemed too suburban, too gentile, and not gritty enough. I didn't want to be Sherlock Holmes. Come to think of it, those two had a lot in common. "The game's afoot!" The adventure and the puzzle. They were not haunted by their cases or plagued by bad dreams. I don't think Nancy had a substance abuse problem. She was high on life. I didn't want to be Sam Spade or Hercule Poirot or Andy Dalziel or Inspector Lloyd or Commander Dalgleish or any of that lot.

I want to be Lew Archer. I want to wake up in my office on a broken-down foldout couch in my underwear and look around in vain for fresh coffee grounds, and, finally resigned to my fate, rummage around in the trash can to find yesterday's filters. I want to fight for the desperate innocents, attractive and unattractive, who turn out not to be quite so guileless or guiltless and in the course of things be arrested and

12

knocked out and tied to a pipe in a flooded basement and get the girl and lose her and make jokes along the way and wryly admit at the end that things are not as they seem and justice is stumbling blind and corrupt. I have always wanted to be a detective.

What to do with all those bonus years

Now that we are over the shock at being told by the media that we have twenty or thirty years more to live, in more or less good health and with more brain function than we thought we would still have by now plus untapped creativity and energy, we'd better find something great to do with these years before we are suddenly eighty-five and we go downhill faster than the Jamaican bobsled team.

I have an idea. I don't really feel a need to go back to school and become an opera singer or a chiropractor or even a dog whisperer, but I think I can pick up a little extra change to cover my recent vices like having to have private swing-dance lessons, private Pilates lessons, and to purchase French shoes more often than other women. Did you know that my feet are exactly the right shape to wear French shoes? Not Italian. I am saved the expense of Ferragamos and I think they're kind of frumpy anyway. As I say, I need a little extra cash. Did I mention I eat all my meals out?

So here's my idea. Many people will want to start new careers, but they are hampered by not having the proper degree or experience or maybe no experience. I will offer to write or fabricate as much of their résumé as they need for a particular opening.

By the time the powers that be get wise to them, they'll be really old and ready to retire. It's not like anyone is going to apply to be president of Harvard or a translator of obscure languages for the U.N. Because if you get caught lying about your credentials in that kind of job, it makes the papers and embarrasses your grandchildren.

Say you're like my friend Sidelle. She woke up one morning and realized that she was too old to start a career as a welder of massive outdoor steel sculpture, but she thinks she might be really terrific as an outsider artist. She asks me to prepare an artist statement and résumé for her new career. I do.

SIDELLE MISNICK
ARTIST'S STATEMENT/RÉSUMÉ

Listen, I've always been an outsider artist . . . before it got religion. Here's the thing: I would put the kids to sleep and then I'd go to the backyard and smoke, and I'd do a little painting. Yes, from my head, things I imagined. Sometimes I'd paint while the laundry was in the dryer. I painted in the Laundromat.

After a while people would come by to see my paintings. It was like, "Let's get a pizza and see what Sidelle's up to." Then I had a show at the Guggenheim. No biggie. They just came by one day and asked me. Yes, painting has sustained me through a difficult life . . . that and a joint.

Then she thinks it might be more professional if I make up a list of her exhibits. I do.

And then, just in case she has to fall back on teaching, I give her a PhD from The Little College under the Volcano, Samoa. I can do the same for you.

Wait! I hear my vocation calling: <u>Catcher in the Rye</u> for adults

Today I have to renew my license at the DMV, conveniently located in a neighborhood I never visit, on an angled street that I never use. I know that I will get lost, and should I fail the exam I will have to console myself by myself.

I would pay anything to a companion for the trip to the DMV. One who would drive, sit with me waiting for my number to be called, and say something witty while my photo is being taken. My mother cut her picture out of her license because it was unattractive. When she was in Disneyland getting over my father's death, a car hit her even though she was on the sidewalk. When the police came, they were horrified that she had cut her photo out of her license. She said, "Officers, I'm the victim here." And I believe that settled the matter.

Yes, it helps to have money at this time in your life. It's easier to make large changes if you don't really need money. Perhaps you could be one of those people who's so embarrassing to their families that they are paid to stay away. Perhaps that has only happened in movies. On the other hand, my plan, the providing of personal loving assistants, has the benefit of offering interesting, highly paid work to those who must work and a wonderful companion to those who were smart enough not to have put all their assets into tech stocks, while also leaving room for the middleman who can bring the two of you together.

I think personal services are the new growth industry. From people who organize your closets and hold your hand while you part with a pair of boots you never liked to those who hold up tiny color swatches in your kitchen and never get cranky doing it.

Don't tell me that you're sick of caretaking and that you've spent thirty years catering to your husband and kids. I'm talking about not only getting paid for doing the little things, but getting the kind of profuse thanks that only another sixty-year-old can give you.

Here are some of the things that I want someone to do with me: Drive across country and visit all the little towns on the way and suss out cafés with eatable food. Someone to fly with me and deal with the hell that is air travel in Italy, who will bring me coffee and keep checking with the desk to find out if our gate has been changed or the flight canceled, and who will call ahead to Amsterdam to alert the bed and breakfast that we will be very late.

And don't tell me smugly that if one has the good fortune to be married, one's husband will lighten the difficulties of travel. My God, I'm surprised you can say it with a straight face.

My husband considered a road trip as a series of stops allowing him to study the route to the next stop. He had a fear of flying. He was white-knuckled at all arrivals and departures, he had migraine headaches, and while I had no control of the money, I had to keep the checkbook. On one memorable trip, he made me walk down a steep hill because taking the ski lift up had shaken him badly and the trip down was too awful to contemplate. Your husband, even if he is still around the house, is not going to want to do the things that a paid companion will do happily and competently.

Remember Judith Anderson as the loyal housekeeper in *Rebecca*? Would anyone you know be willing to burn down Manderley Hall just to honor your memory or have a spine so straight you could bowl on it? I think not.

I would pay the earth to have someone bring me a cup of coffee in the morning from the café down the street, the way I like it, feed the cats who begin screaming as soon as the sun comes up, and sweet-talk me out of bed. "You're great. The war in Iraq is winding down. The world needs you. Get out of bed, put one foot down. See, you can do it." And make the bed as soon as I'm out of it. He or she can go on to work or whatever afterwards.

Did you know that one of Picasso's wives would prepare a copy of the painting he was working on so that he could take the work in two different directions simultaneously?

I have projects too. I would like them to be treated with the same respect Françoise gave Pablo's.

Things I will never do

Okay, sixty is the new forty. Old age doesn't start when we thought it did. Now it's mandatory to become a second-wind achiever. Just what I needed, more stress, more pressure.

I had my plans set. I was thinking about breaking in a new housedress, a tight perm, and riding the backs of my fluffy house shoes down until they were backless. I planned to perfect my shuffle from the living room, where the TV is, to the kitchen and back, with a quick pit stop at my bathroom with metal rails strategically placed.

Oh, rats, now it turns out we've got a bunch of bonus years . . . we're not officially old until eighty-five. Don't worry; technology is so advanced that your kitchen timer will go off when you reach old age. You'll get a big party when you hit ninety and then it's off to the ice floe for you. So enjoy it. Max out your credit cards; take out a thirty-year mortgage on a beach house.

What are we going to do with the next three or four decades? There's an expectation that we will do something exceptional, better than we did the first time around. Between keeping Alzheimer's at bay and being physically fit and attractive and healthy, we're expected to build a new fulfilling life on the foundation of our past. Let me at least shove some stuff out of sight; give me time to put a bucket under the leak.

Certain things, though, it's too late to do

I will never ride a horse across the desert, swim the English Channel, or play Grace Kelly in the movie of her life.

Inline skating is closed to me, as is a medical career. I will not ride in a demolition derby or drive a Porsche on the autobahn. I will not dine on camel tongue or eat that fish in Japan that gives you a poisonous buzz or herd cattle or play the machines in a casino called something like the *Delta Queen* and wink at the guy who just hit the jackpot on the quarter slots and leave the same night to get married in Las Vegas at the Elvis Chapel because that is something it turns out that both of us have always wanted to do.

On the other hand, it's also way too late for me to give birth to someone who will grow up to be a serial killer or the spokesperson for a large company which has just done something unspeakable to the environment.

In fact, as many books tell us, this is the time in my life when I can concentrate on being me, when the responsibilities of being a wife and mother are behind me. Yes, I know it's hard to believe, but I was married once and have three children. Well, the second part is a lie, but you get my drift. I now have the leisure to reevaluate my life and time to change it. Thank God it's too late to be the first female tourist in space.

I'm discussing aging with a stranger in a bookstore and she says, "I'm just glad I can put one foot in front of the other." I hiss at her. "Wake up," I say. "This is the moment for your epiphany, and the one where you decide you have always wanted to climb a huge mountain in a place far away." "Well," she says, "I've always hated my teeth." "Yes," I exult, "you can now wear braces that are invisible to the naked eye and in thirty-six months you can have perfect teeth and the smile you always wanted." I didn't mention that you can't eat

19

while wearing them, so the idea of a spontaneous snack of three chicken flautas is out, and that they and your teeth must be brushed before putting them back in. But she'll find that out soon enough and the important thing is that she's doing something to change her life.

In my family, reading the classifieds took the place of organized religion. We were always on the lookout for a better job, or in my father's case, another business opportunity. I was so enamored of the want ads that when I became a feminist, the first action I joined was a suit against gender-segregated classifieds. We won! No other battle has been as satisfying or clear-cut. Now men can apply for secretarial positions.

Every time I pass the brick house with the wonderful screened-in porch where the lights are bright and beckoning and where they hold daily AA meetings and where groups of fairly attractive people are standing outside smoking and talking . . . I wish it wasn't too late to become an alcoholic.

Minor disturbances in the field

I meet the grandchild of an old friend. She is around six and has extraordinary charisma; she's physically fearless, able to engage with strangers immediately, and is totally present. I wish she were mine. This doesn't make me rethink my decision not to have children, but it does rock my world for a moment.

I will find something to be grateful for every day, just like they tell you to do in self-help books

I have been longing to be sixty-five and eligible for Medicare. It's everything they promised and more. I love my prescription plan too. It serves me well, because I have nothing complicated wrong with me, just the usual. If, of course, I suddenly developed something serious, it might turn out that I had picked the wrong plan and I would get a letter advising me that my drug was not in their formulary and that I would have to forgo it or pay cash.

Activities to take the place of tennis when you're older

Get a group of girlfriends together and set them the assignment to find the best tiramisu in the city. When that activity pales, as it will, the group can research key lime pie and then cheesecake. It's amazing how these tried-and-true desserts can vary in flavor, texture, and consistency. When this activity pales, move it to another town or start sampling baba ghanoushes or polenta.

Now that we are in our sixties, even lying is better

Remember how we hurt people's feelings in high school before we developed empathy and before professional lying organizations existed? In the olden days, if an undesirable boy asked you to the big dance and your mind was screaming, "Get him away from me, make this not be happening! Oh, my God, think of something to say, but not 'How dare you ask me out, geek boy,' " followed by the highly undesirable and painful thought: "If a geek asks me out, am I also a geek? Yes, I am. Oh, my God! Help me!"

We were primitive then, but even back then, I knew I couldn't say I was washing my hair—the prom was too far away—so with the quick thinking that I am known for, I said, "I've been exposed to measles and I should have a full-blown case by prom night." Okay, I tremble thinking of that awful girl, and that poor boy. Things are different now. He's become a nationally known writer; maybe it's time to look him up.

We now have the technology to lie in a professional manner. Our lying can be assisted by online service companies who provide professional alibis. I think there's room for one more service and I think I can get seed money for a website and other start-up costs. Yes, this is what I'm going to do with those bonus years of energy and creativity that the media promises will start just about now! The sixties are the new forties. Go for it!

If these companies had existed then, I would have been a charter member. I could have said yes to the boy, made him feel good, and quickly arranged on my cell phone (what did we do before cell phones?) to be called to the principal's office and then taken out of school that very day. "Please come to the office, Ms. Garrison. Emergency! Will someone find Miss Nikki Garrison and tell her the CCD in Georgia is on the line. Her house has been quarantined and she must return home immediately. She must go directly home! All students are advised to avoid contact! The janitorial staff will proceed to decontaminate her homeroom. We would like you all to come to grief counseling later today to work out your feelings for Nikki, which I am sure are somewhat ambiguous. Students, do you remember that movie where the young couple goes to Paris on their honeymoon and the adorable husband goes downstairs to get a pack of cigarettes and when he comes back no one has heard of his wife and the room has been completely redecorated? That's sort of what's happened to your beloved fellow student, whom a few of you may actually know."

What a face-saving, benevolent service that would have been. So much preferable to devastating a perfectly innocent lad. We are so lucky to be able to avail ourselves of that service now. No need for your mate to know you've been having a temporary leave of your senses with your personal trainer. . . . No, you're away at a conference. Perhaps you're the keynote speaker.

This company can even arrange to have your image inserted into the group photos of the conference attendees. Photoshop is part of the solution. Kinkos can make your groundbreaking speech available in a single-copy bound remembrance, with a separate four-color cover. . . . Or perhaps on a DVD if money is no object. Emergency telephone numbers can be provided, with twenty-four-hour operators on call to say you've just stepped out for a snack.

Say your needs are more modest. You're at a party, a family gathering, or a real business meeting and you feel the top of your head will blow off if you have to stay a moment longer. Just press *Get me out of here* on speed dial and one of our operators will call back providing you with one of three suitable emergency messages: your husband has just had a heart attack—don't worry, it's a tiny one, more of a panic attack really—or your wife has just delivered a ten-pound baby boy, a miracle, since she's sixty if she's a day, or your house is on fire.

Daily expressions of gratitude: the chocolate, espresso, and vodka martini for the soul

Yes, women have been honored for their contributions to science and culture, and to the betterment of other women's lives. I'm not denying it. We laud Madame Curie and the woman who invented correction fluid . . . she was the mother of one of the Monkees. Every time a bride drops a red M&M on her dress and uses Liquid Paper, she calls out the name Bette Nesmith Graham and blesses her. And we praise the Widow Clicquot, who made quality clarified champagne possible.

But what of the women who are little known? Shouldn't they be honored for the small ways in which they made our lives better? The woman who noticed that mascara works admirably to hide those first gray hairs; the first woman to use paper clips and/or masking tape to fix a hem; the woman who used chewing gum to keep a pesky bra strap in place, nail polish to stop a run. . . . It's not too late to invent something simple and useful. Women hold 10 percent of the world's patents. They think up lots of things in Indonesia. I Google inventions by women. They range from stuff you use on space shuttles to my favorite: plastic coverings for shoes, attached by rubber bands to keep the shoes of food-service people from being covered with gunk.

"Think small," I tell the girlfriend. "Someone had to invent that metal thingy you put over your frying pan to keep the spaghetti sauce from spraying your oven top. Lint rollers, think of the beauty and simplicity of that idea. I'd like to design a slipcover for my clothing, something beautiful, and disposable, so no one would say, 'Jeez, that woman's wearing a bib, she should be kept out of sight.' " Given the amount of fuss people throw over seeing a woman breast-feed in public, I don't suppose I could just remove my blouse at dinner. I've seen men at lunch throwing their ties over their shoulders so they don't stain them. Who was the first man to come up with that solution? He deserves a bronze statue. You wouldn't even have to put his name on it, just show his tie nonchalantly thrown over his shoulder and a forkful of spaghetti halfway to his mouth.

Bad habits: smoke that cigarette

I am at Audrey's house. She is smoking. "When did you start that?" I ask.

"What the hell," she cackles, "I am sixty. I am going to start smoking."

I say, "If you want to kill yourself, heroin or crack or perhaps crank would be more amusing, right?"

She says: "You think I am doing this for myself?" I am immediately ashamed. I hang my head in anticipation of her reasoning, which will make me feel I am an unfeeling piece of garbage.

"I am using myself as a human sacrifice and I am starting a movement. You will join my movement and others will join and soon many women over forty will be smoking. We will form a multitude." She laid it out:

Newsmakers will take note of this trend and our images will flood the media. We will be interviewed. We will smoke on cable and a video of us will circulate on the Internet. Concerned parents will TiVo our appearances. *Frontline* will make a very good documentary about us. Some of us will even stuff wads of snuff into our mouths and let a stream of brown juice run down our chins. Many young people who are not deterred by the thought of their early death from lung cancer will see unattractive old people smoking and they will be repulsed. Cigarettes will drop from pubescent lips all over the country. By the time we are no longer a media event, those children will have reached eighteen and you know if you don't smoke by the time you have reached eighteen, chances are you never will. It will be the final blow to the tobacco industry.

She hands me a cigarette and a rather elegant lighter. "Save the children." I light up and notify my broker to sell my tobacco stock.

Take my hand; I'm a stranger in paradise

Perhaps I can get a foundation grant in my bonus years, one that finances the services that are so badly needed in our age of machines that confuse and confound those over forty. The parking lot at my favorite movie theater is now completely automated. There are no attendants. You must pay for your parking in the theater building before you get into your car or you will never get out of the parking lot. A recorded message to that effect is loudly delivered over and over again as I search for a spot. I was in line to pay when I noticed that the woman in front of me was having a problem. She had not figured out that the ticket goes in the same slot as the credit card. I explained this to her. "Thanks," she said, and then, "Oh, damn, I forgot to get the ticket stamped."

Under the terms of my grant, I'll stand beside the CTA card reader at the train station to explain the intricacies of adding value to your card, to show you when to press *Vend,* and to make sure that your dollar bill is facing up so that the president's face and not the White House goes into the slot. I would straighten the bill if it was too crumpled to be accepted by the machine.

When I was not needed at the machine, I would move to the gate to make sure you put your card in with the arrow pointing in the correct direction. Lots of time is wasted turning one's card around and around in that slot, while those behind you say rude things and you get confused. I know. I've been there. I could bring empathy to the job.

I would be prepared, if compensated well enough, to carry a beeper around with me and rush to the aid of those who are flummoxed by drive-through windows, ATM machines, and navigating the rapids of online traffic school without abandoning the site the first time it takes you back to where you started and you lose everything. (When I was interested in meeting men, I briefly considered going to real traffic school, where I could meet men with whom I had a lot in common, in a natural situation, as opposed to a bar. I'm sure many of them had been, like me, tagged for sliding through a stop sign, which makes us compatible, but it meant going downtown, so I gave it a pass.)

I could help people use the handheld scanner at grocery stores. This marvelous device was discontinued at my local market because only 129 people used it during the first six months. I could have guided shoppers through the initial learning curve. I would also be available to help the indecisive: Are you wondering whether to buy a house or a condo, to order the fish or the lamb? Just beep me.

I hear someone whining, Well, what about setting up my TiVo, stereo, DVD, or my grandchild's four-poster canopied bed?

I acknowledge that those particular skills are beyond me. However, I promise to hire a crew of cute, funny guys who will drop everything to be at your side when you beep. Hand them a $50 bill and a six-pack as they come in, and go read a mystery. Remember how you could never read while the man in your life set up the stereo system? You had to remain in the room and look as attentive as Nancy Reagan standing next to Ron during his campaigns.

Here's a really nice job for someone just hanging around the house, dying for something to do, that involves travel. How does working as a stand-in look-alike for a political wife sound? You're saying, How hard could it be? I'm sure most wives of politicians would rather be learning how to skateboard or having their legs waxed than staring seriously for long periods of time at their husband while he speaks in gross generalities about important political issues. Big yawn. This stand-in role would be a great job for a recent retiree who likes to travel, and what woman wouldn't want to see small towns, dress up in someone else's clothes, and get a free haircut? Send me your headshot; I'll see what I can do.

Girls just want to have fun

What if you don't want to be productive? What if you say the hell with it, I want an unusual hobby and don't suggest those paint-by-number things, the new ones use very light ink and the spaces are too small to fill in neatly.

I tell the girlfriends that I am an expert on hobbies and obsession. I have been collecting graphically interesting condom packaging and containers for years. Amsterdam package designers are the best and their condoms can be purchased online. Not that Amsterdam isn't a great city to visit.

Once I went into a sex store in Paris, where the clerks were larger than any Frenchmen I had even seen and the walls were covered with television sets running grotesque sex videos. I asked for condoms in my rather rudimentary French, but I was immediately distracted by a German cream that was beautifully packaged in black and pink, an art deco silhouette of a woman on the front. Her body had a highlight on the spot where the cream was to be best used, like you might get confused and put it on your feet. I pointed to the container. The huge thuglike clerk held out another to me and said, "This one's better." I explained that I was only interested in graphic superiority and he raised an eyebrow that signifies the world over: "Right, lady, tell me another."

I know that someday when condoms are an amusing memory and the ingredient that prevents pregnancy and disease is available as a gelato in green tea, rocky road, and strawberry flavors, my condom collection will be worth a fortune as an exotic curiosity.

Each of the girlfriends has her own obsession, which she

insists is a collection and not a sign of dementia. Each firmly believes that there will be frenzied bidding for her collection and her windfall will make her old age easy and pleasant. Bitsy collects handbags. She has rented an apartment just for the extra closet space it affords her. The kitchen cabinets are filled with purses as well. Sally collects poodle images and poodle sculpture. She has a poodle museum in her basement. My collection has the advantage over theirs of being compact enough to fit in two drawers and a hatbox . . . protected from the sun and dust-free until several people make frenzied attempts to buy it.

Chapter 2 When I am old, I will Live in a Castle

Not just a roof over my head, but a vaulted ceiling

Sally and Bitsy and I are screaming at each other. It all started when Sally said that drinking eight glasses of water a day was a crock and Bitsy said Sally had thrown her vote away on Nader and I said I can't stand the way Bitsy's kitchen makes a snake pit look organized, when I decide this is the proper moment to bring up how we will all live together when we are old.

Sally says, "What about our husbands?" Sally is the only one who has a husband. I say, "If you die before George, he will be part of our commune, because he is handy and neat." Okay, that's settled. "And what about the dogs and cats?" "They will have their own condo," I say, my fingers crossed.

"Where are we going to live?" "Indiana," says Sally. "Key West," says Bitsy. "French Riviera," I say. Okay, let's leave that for the moment. Do we live in an apartment or a condo? Do we have live-in help? I say, "I want to live in a big city, in a huge apartment complex with its own grocery, movie theaters, and putting green, and a number of really fine restaurants."

Sally says she pictures us all sitting on the front porch of her family home in Indiana. We are in rocking chairs and knitting long scarves for flood victims . . . somewhere. "Sally," I ask pleasantly, "do you see me coming up behind you and rocking you so fast and so hard that you fly off the porch and land in a briar patch, and I leave you there?"

33

Sally begins to cry. Bitsy hisses at me. I run off to locate my journal in which I know I have written about each of them and the reasons why they are still in my life. I can't find it, but I remember the times they have told me I was wonderful and held my hand, when thousands wouldn't.

I come back into the room. I gather them in my arms. They beam at me, little lambs that they are, and I say, "Sally, we can have rocking chairs on the condo balcony, and Bitsy, you can grow a few palm trees in buckets." There is silence. I decide to up the ante. "Once a week we'll have dirty martinis and chili cheese fries for dinner." They unmelt slightly.

I bring out an article about ten old friends who decide to build individual homes on a piece of land that they own together. "Imagine the difficulties they had to overcome to stay with that project," I say. One of the big sticking points was that some people wanted the trim to be the color of eggplant. "I like eggplant," says Sally. "As much as having your own reflexologist?" I ask. She smiles and I feel the sun on my face and a world full of possibilities. "Are you wearing sun screen?" asks Bitsy. "Yes," I lie. "It's got an SPF of a hundred fifty. It also protects me against UV rays and alien abduction."

Secondary sources: hobbies for the extremely wealthy

I have been reading books on the subject of retirement. They aim to be a road map for jolly and fulfilling old age. They are often brightly illustrated and arranged alphabetically for ease in choosing among the many appealing ideas.

I have a favorite: Buying a castle in Europe and converting

it into an art gallery. Or if your soul will only be nourished by the idea of helping the less fortunate, turning it into a pet shelter. Personally I would buy that castle and turn it into a salon, call it The Nail Hut and be the only nail salon in the Loire Valley. Start a franchise, bringing sculptured nails to tiny outposts of civilization. Give the world a pedicure.

I was so intrigued that I looked up castles for sale or rent and found it was as I thought: there were no real bargains. Most of those offered were in the $3 million range and what with putting up new wallboard, painting, and lawn care, we're talking big money. I can't run down to the café and interest one or two of my pals in investing in a castle. I can't even imagine how the girlfriends would react. I would need at least fifty investors. Actually, that's not impossible. Maybe next time I go to the Green Dolphin, where people are drinking and dancing, I will make my pitch.

Hobbies for the extremely wealthy who like to serve on boards for worthy causes

Realizing that the housing options for ordinary people who have devoted their lives to the arts and thus sacrificed the opportunity to be asked to join corporate boards and be paid barrels of money and are now in sort of a tight spot, financially, are few, you and your pals might set up a foundation to address this problem. Contact a developer you know, or join an advisory board to discuss alternative rental housing.

I was trying to beat my time in reading the entire *New York Times* without retaining anything, when my eye was caught by an article about a group of older people in the arts who were living in an apartment building developed with their needs in mind. (The definition of the arts was elastic, which I liked . . . hair stylists for the stars and people who trained dogs for sitcom roles were included.)

They were living together and keeping each other vibrant and alive by their common interests and by the sometimes edgy, competitive atmosphere that surrounds those of us who are committed to spirituality and artistic expression. This experiment in living was in California.

I have already changed my plan. I don't see why I have to think big. How about getting five people together to build something perfect for community living. I'm already dreaming about the blueprints, placing the elevators, the greenhouse, and the extra kitchens. Seven bedrooms, seven and a half baths, a dance hall, and a fifty-seat auditorium. This will keep me occupied for some time.

Every day send a wish out to the universe: Today wish for the pot of gold at the end of the rainbow

Today I'm hoping that someone else with more energy and persistence than I possess is also thinking about alternative housing for artists and that when she comes up with a proposal, I am asked to be one of the first tenants.

Old hobbies die hard

I run into Joy and her husband in the coffee shop on Sunday. He tells me that the Dustin Hoffman movie that she was an extra in is coming out. Her part had gotten bigger when they discovered she could swim. In one scene she swims and in another, she comes out of the pool. Her husband takes the dogs home and we continue talking as we walk down the street. We stop short when we notice a realtor's sign for an open house. She admits that she is addicted to looking at houses. "Me, too," I say. We walk in; the realtor takes one look at how we're dressed and continues to talk on her cell. The house is enormous. It has countless bedrooms, numerous decks, and no yard. It's on the market for $1.74 million. We agree it could be easily converted into a commune for our aged friends and us. That's next week's project. I haven't forgotten that I need to find a way to put my telephone number on my glasses, along with the word *Reward*. I still have two pairs, and haven't lost the old pair, but it's only a matter of time.

Today my assistant carefully wrote my telephone number and the word *Reward* on pieces of white tape and attached them it to the stems of my glasses. This should solve all my problems.

Hobbies for regular people

Remarry. Try someone new for twenty-five years. See how many times you can fit marriage into one lifetime. Renew your vows after a month. Take a vow of silence. (Remember how attractive that made Holly Hunter in *The Piano*.) Learn sign language.

Collect those old machines that kids used to put their feet into when trying on new shoes. Remember when the green light went on you could see the bones in your feet? Shoe shopping was an event kids looked forward to. You can start a conversation with any stranger of a certain age by mentioning those machines. Or plastic bubble medium that came in a small tube. You could blow a bubble with it, or, if you were a boy, you might eat it.

Commercial applications for your collection: that X-ray machine could be placed anywhere that bored men sit, glassy-eyed, waiting for their significant other to finish shopping. To activate it you'd have to feed it quarters. It would only work for so long and then you'd have to feed it again. Like a parking meter in a busy area, only even more of a holdup: a quarter for thirty seconds. ATM machines could be placed nearby for convenience. I wonder if I could get an ATM machine at my front door? Or in the garden? So convenient for me and my neighbors and an extra source of income. How to present this to my neighbors without alarming them?

Childish hobbies that alas cannot be repeated as a grownup, because they would be way weird

When I was a little girl, my maternal grandmother often took care of me. I would amuse myself with paper dolls that I played with in the space behind the Murphy bed. On Sundays we tuned in to a sad radio program called *The Eternal Light.*

The program was heart-wrenching. We would all cry. Sometimes to break the spell, my grandfather would tickle the bottom of my foot with a shoehorn.

My grandmother and I would often bathe together and she invented a game called "The Titanic." We would fill the tub to the brim and she'd splash around making the water move violently in waves and I would be tossed from side to side while she held me safely in her huge arms and shouted: "We're sinking! Save the women and children first! Save the women and children first!" How I miss that game.

Every day find something new to be grateful for: Kama Sutra for the soul

One of the Pilates instructors that I have enlisted to bring me positive stories of aging told me that due to a set of unavoidable circumstances she and her boyfriend could not use his apartment or hers and were forced to have sex in the back seat of her car. Afterwards he revealed that he had never done it in a car before. I expressed surprise. "He's from Chicago, isn't he? Of course he's done it in a car. It's not like he's a New Yorker." Think of all the places you've never had sex in or at. Make a list. Cross those places off the list when you have accomplished your task. Do not cheat.

People steal my ideas

I call the girlfriends on speakerphone. "It happened again," I rant. "Someone stole my idea!"

"Which one?" Bitsy asks. "The Farm Aid concert or the dog whisperer/psychic hotline?"

"My bookstore idea! Remember how I used to watch that stupid program *Banacek* because at one point in every show he goes to his friend Felix Mulholland's antiquarian bookstore to consult him on a case or make a brilliant chess move? Do you remember the shop, more like a gallery, really? It had two stories, the second reached by a beautiful wooden circular staircase. . . . Wood! There wasn't a bit of plastic in the place and no cash registers and no customers either. Did having no customers trouble Felix? No, he was not troubled! Customers would be a nuisance, taking him away from his engrossing research, the specifics of which were never given, and who cares?"

When *Banacek* went off the air I gave up my fantasy of opening a bookstore. I still collect paperback mysteries . . . stuffing them here and there . . . in the closet, under the bed, in the medicine chest . . . in case I open up a used mystery bookstore. Felix Mulholland, of course, had no paperbacks sullying his antiquarian shelves.

"And now Garrison Keillor is opening a bookstore in St. Paul. He's sixty-four, he just had surgery to prevent further strokes, and he's started a novel. Don't tell me that order is accidental. And now I can't open a bookstore because he has one."

Audrey says, "There's room for more than one bookstore, especially if they are in different states."

"Thank you for reminding me, Audrey." I am sincere. "This is perfect," I say. "Because there's an available space in the building down the block. It was going to be a liquor store, but neighborhood people complained and now it's free again. We could have terrific fun making it a replica of the one on *Banacek,* and then of course we'd go to book fairs, meet authors, and get a lot of free books. My God, there's a lot to do before we open."

"Could we sell hotdogs?" Bitsy asks. "I've never seen a

40

bookstore/Vienna hotdog stand combination. I'm sure it'd be a big draw, especially in the city that invented piccalilli." We're all excited and go to have lunch to talk over the details.

Where has my nest egg gone?

I am convening a weekend seminar, in the Bahamas, to help people prepare their rationalizations and apologies for various things done and undone to their children and heirs. In place of a will, join a famous director and others like yourself to prepare a DVD showing your children and grandchildren what you did with their inheritance. Take them on a virtual tour of your life, go to the garage, show them the cars, show them the in-ground swimming pool, the pool boy, and memorabilia of exotic vacations. Explain why you had to have a flat screen TV. One that turns into a mirror when it's off. Anticipate their howls of "When was it ever off?"

If still alive and out of money recite the reasons why you spent your nest egg. Recite your rationalizations poetically and explain in detail why you can't possibly live with them, why you must have a stipend in order to afford your own place. Do not mention that their house is too small to encompass your theater system, a system so good that your image at home can exceed the ones at movie houses, as long as you keep upgrading your electronic equipment. Tell them you have to go to Italy to learn how to cook healthy low-fat antioxidant meals. Tell them you think you're pregnant. Whether it's for a full-time aesthetician or a wine cellar, our editors can make your need sound credible.

Going shopping when you're old

Sally shows us two pale yellow identical cashmere sweaters she just bought. "Why?" I ask. "You have more clothes than you'll ever need. Why would you buy more?" I myself have dropped clothing in those ubiquitous Gaia boxes and taken others to a consignment shop and I still have more than I could ever use. Not to speak of elegant dresses that I will never wear because I am not invited to those kinds of events and even at those events you can wear blue jeans. Have you noticed that even at the most elegant restaurants, women are in T-shirts?

Which leads me to the philosophy that I have developed over a period of minutes.

The girlfriends lean forward, eyes gleaming with anticipation to catch the pearls of wisdom that I am about to drop. Perhaps that is an exaggeration. Sally lets her eyes roll back in her head and Bitsy studies her nails in resignation.

"I'm going to start a foundation. Let's call it the Harry Winston Foundation. The young will pay into it, like Social Security. And instead of receiving some paltry amount in their early seventies they will have the satisfaction of knowing that some wrinkled old woman and her pals are sitting on the front porch of some dilapidated farmhouse in Costa Rica wearing a fortune in diamonds. Thanks, young people."

Bitsy whispers, "You've left something out. Death."

"First of all, death has nothing to do with shopping," I say. (I couldn't have been more wrong.)

"We've agreed on cremation. My ashes will be in a vintage cookie tin, Bitsy's in a mason jar, and Sally is willing to join

42

any of us in our containers as long as there's no fighting! So there'll be some Tuva throat singing and then our ashes will be emptied from one of the cliffs of Dover into the sea. Very touching. Sally is also going to write our death announcement in French and English, so that it runs in a number of international papers. We'll have a big memorial event at a hotel downtown with a swing band and dancing and later a wake at the Everest Room. Everyone drinks a toast to me with red Lillet. If it's Bitsy, a dirty martini with five olives, and if it's Sally, they toast with whatever weirdly sweet drink is in, and then we'll bring the drugs out."

Bitsy is shaking her head. "You are like so nineties. Do you know the average amount of ashes that blow back into the mourners' faces is equal to an atomic blast, not to speak of the unspeakable stuff mixed in with the ashes to fill up the urn—cigar ends and mite dust?"

"Stop," I beg. "Just tell me the newest in thing in burials and I will write it into my will."

"Huge mausoleums," she says. "Loft-size, above-ground memorials with fireplaces and ceiling fans and gas grills and koi ponds with marble terraces and a great view and huge mobile homes for your family to stay in when they come to lay flowers or angry notes on your grave."

"What's this about mobile homes?" I ask. "No one I know wants a mobile home." "They're fabulous now," she says, "in gated trailer parks." She waves a blueprint under my nose. "Sniff it," she says. I do, and it smells large and expensive. "Tell me more," I say. "They're enormous, big as a football field and they come in colonial, ranch, or mini-mansion. They run about $700,000 and that's not counting the land, which is $250,000 and a bargain because of the golf courses and the pool."

I don't want to admit it, but I am dying to see photos. Bitsy slyly takes out a brochure. We gather round. "You'll notice that the living area has plenty of storage space," she says, looking meaningfully at me. "It even has panels that fold out so that you can watch TV outside, sheltered from the elements."

"Folks can drop by and watch what you're watching and have a cool drink and something grilled." This sounds perfect because any arrangement involving more than one friend necessitates ten phone calls to find the right day, time, week, and decade to meet.

"Yes," says Bitsy, and hands me the clincher: "You don't have to leave home. Your guests come to you." I'm in, as long as the trailer never moves from its hookups.

"Okay, is there anything else left to buy?"

They lean in toward me. For the first time I notice their hair. It seems thicker, like Joe Biden's.

"Implants," they say, beaming in unison. "And did you know that seventy-five to eighty percent of women are wearing the wrong size bra, so we need to go bra shopping, too."

"Will a new properly fitted bra raise my breasts to the level they were when I was sixteen?" I ask hopefully. "When you were sixteen you wore them right under your clavicle," Sally says disapprovingly. "It looked unnatural then and worse now."

"Okay, I'll get fitted for new bras as long as they are very, very expensive," I say. "And I have no need for hair implants since I have thick, naturally wavy hair." "Yeah, we know," they say. "Your hair is so fabulous that people come up to you on the street and curtsy." They roll their eyes and we go out to get fitted.

We enter the bra boutique. It is full of young women selling bras and other young women buying items from a wedding registry. Now one can register at a lingerie store. I briefly consider getting married again. I was intensely moral and austere when I got married and refused a bridal shower.... Moral, austere, and blindingly stupid.

One of the young women asks if I want help. She will fit me with the correct bra size. We have been bombarded with articles about how we have all been wearing the wrong bra size and promised that as soon as we are fitted, our breasts will look perky again and also smooth under our skimpy T-shirts. Sally has wandered over to the wedding section and is fingering T-shirts that have BRIDE written across the chest in sequins. Bitsy is over in the expensive area, looking at the lingerie that *Sex and the City* made popular. I pull them away and direct them to the striptease section, full of red garter belts and little coupon books full of detachable permissions for tantalizing acts, to give to your beloved.

I am fitted. Disappointingly enough I am wearing the correct size, but I fill the fantasy gap by buying two very expensive French bras, one in black and one in nude. They are ever so slightly padded, giving me a smooth line under my summer tees. I do not buy the special washing solution that will add to the life of the bra. I do not need it to last longer than I do.

Sometime later I experience a slight wardrobe malfunction. I am standing, vigorously making a point about hot stone massages, and I feel my breasts start to creep out from under my bra. I am so stunned that I sit down in mid-sentence.

I return to the shop and ask to be refitted. I am measured. I try on various lovely creations. One has little flowers in place of straps. The flower straps cannot be adjusted; one would have to find a little seamstress to take them in. I forgo the daisies.

Suddenly enormous bras fill the room. I have become a 34D! Must be the Pilates. I ask how I could have changed bra sizes when my original fitting, at the same boutique, was just a few months ago. How could this possibly be true? Is it a surprise pregnancy? A very localized weight gain? The computer is consulted. The name of the previous fitter is revealed as someone who is no longer there, an inferior fitter.

I receive 25 percent off the new bras. Big deal. Now I have four new bras, two of which are too small. . . . Although the two earlier ones work perfectly well if I am lying still, reading.

I call an old flame to give him the good news: I am now a 34D. He will make a special trip in the fall to see the new me. Perhaps by that time I will be an E.

Let's have a round of applause for the little lady: EMTs for the soul

Remember when there were claques at theaters? Maybe you're not as old as I am. . . . These people came to the theater as a group and applauded wildly for the actor who had hired them. I think we need a claque in daily life. Perhaps it's not necessary that they follow you around to applaud your little victories, maybe you can wait and tell them later. . . . No, I take that back, I want an immediate response. Like that fast-food chain in Indiana, Hot 'N Now is how I want it.

I call another meeting of the board of the Harry Winston Foundation

I feel we have to widen our mission. We have to be more proactive in raising funds for the foundation. First of all, last week I realized that winter would soon be here and I would be even more reluctant to drive than I am now. Last week I went to a haiku poetry slam and because it was located in a venue in an intersection where three, count them three, angled streets come together, I decided to take a taxi. And that made me think about all the other women who need to take taxis so that their cultural life will flourish rather than wither. Sally asks, "Is the foundation specifically geared to catering to your needs?" "You make me sound so selfish," I say. "Do you agree or not that many women over fifty need a foundation grant so that they can take a taxi when they need to increase their exposure to the arts and also to make sure that those arts flourish, because we know that the middle-aged are the majority of the theater-going audience and that theater would die without their participation? I think I can make a very good case for that to some guy like . . . what's the name of that musical guy that I hate? The one that wrote

Les Mis and *Miss Saigon*. Well, anyway, him. I'm sure we can get him to give us a grant." We agree and the meeting is adjourned until one of us gets another really good idea.

Providing for old age

Searching for my roots, I discover I am a Catholic.

"Deborah Kerr had the right idea," I say. "At the end of her career she entered a convent and lived out the remainder of her life being looked after by the good sisters." "Wasn't that a film, with Clint Eastwood?" Bitsy asks. "Or was it the one where she's in a wheelchair and she tries to pretend she's just resting?" "This is real life, Bitsy. And you better start giving it some thought since your nest egg has shriveled," I say, unkindly.

Audrey fixes me with her gimlet eye. "Deborah Kerr was a practicing Catholic. Attending bingo games at St. Ben's does not make you a Catholic. The good sisters are not in your future. Ms. Kerr provided for her old age by sending loads of money to the order. As far as I know, you have never sent any money to sisters of any stripe, your own, feminists, or nuns."

"I'm sure," I say stiffly, "that the nuns will be more forgiving than you are." Anyone is more forgiving than Audrey; Donald Trump being one and Dick Cheney another. "Which nuns did you have in mind?" she asks. "Ingrid Bergman, Whoopi Goldberg, or the singing ones?" "The singing ones are out. As you know, Audrey, I cannot carry a tune." "Perhaps you could just move your lips," Bitsy says sweetly.

I say, "I must find my roots. I have to take a spiritual journey to find some group to take me in, to cosset me and provide a secure home in my old age." "I don't think you have spiritual roots," says Bitsy. "I do too," I say. "I am a spiritual person. I just haven't found my group yet." "Maybe it's the Santerias," Bitsy suggests, "or a group who chants the same phrase over and over . . . good for those of us whose memory is iffy." "What if I found out I was adopted and I show up at my parents' door?" "They would probably be very old and in need of assistance themselves," Audrey points out. "Haven't you ever wanted to find out about the generations before your grandparents?" "That would mean a trip to Russia or Poland," I say, "and that would mean leaving the country. I want to find my roots here, or in Napa Valley, California." The girlfriends agree with alacrity to accompany me on a trip to find my roots. Perhaps I exaggerate about the alacrity. I have to remind them of everything I've done for them in the past and hold my breath and tell them I'll use my miles to pay for the trip or that I'll pay for the hotel room. I'll do whatever is necessary. We're going!

CHAPTER 3

MY Big Birthday

-PLEASE...

LADY, A pie big enough For MORGAN FREEMAN AND JOSH HARTNETT to JUMP OUT OF WOULD HAVE to be reALLy big... Are you sure you DON'T WANT A CAKE?

I'd like schoolchildren and federal employees to get the day off on my birthday

It's my big birthday. I'm Taurus with Leo rising and so I live for the grand gesture and eating all my meals out. I am having my party in a fabulous restaurant in the Big Apple in an elegant room that holds twenty-one comfortably. I begin by inviting the girlfriends, but soon I am aware that the list must be extended. That my choices cannot be based entirely on my own wishes. I hate that.

People make assumptions. They think because they were at my wedding, they are naturally part of any subsequent celebration. I have to set them straight. But at the same time I find myself inviting near strangers because they seem amusing and why not, the room holds twenty-one comfortably. I invite people who live far away. It makes me look good and they won't come.

I am issuing invitations promiscuously. The world suddenly seems filled with potential guests. I have absolutely no room left at the table in the elegant private room of the restaurant where I am having my birthday. And everyone is coming. No one is canceling. In an idle moment I call up Henry Kissinger. Now he's coming too.

It seems I have merely to mention that I am having my birthday in New York and people invite themselves and I seem unable to tell them not to come. I am up to thirty in a room that holds twenty-one comfortably. Someone will cancel. Perhaps a daughter will be delivering her baby or since we are all a certain age, someone will have to have a little surgical procedure.

Now I have reached the stage of remembering old friends who I previously cut out of my life forever. I am sorry I was rash and I want them around me on my birthday. I invite them. I invite people who are kind to me in the grocery store; men who let me cut in front of them on the highway. I fling invitations out the window of my car. I am now up to fifty in the room that holds twenty-one comfortably.

My deposit on the private room is nonrefundable. It's too late to change venues. Ten people have to go. The others will just have to sit a little closer together around the table. It's necessary that ten people have to go . . . one way or another.

I go to my neighborhood bar to pick up a hit man. I have read about hiring hit men in bars in the newspaper. Women go to a neighborhood bar to hire a guy to dispatch their husband and he turns out to be an undercover cop. I hope to be luckier.

I chat with a large hairy man at the bar; he seems trustworthy and he is amenable to paring down my guest list. We arrange another meeting to iron out the details.

Meanwhile, I have made a few adjustments in my appearance. Because I want to look great on my birthday I have acquired perky breasts. And I have a tattoo, a snake wrapped around a heart. And I've cut my hair. But you know how that goes. You start by cutting your hair and then it lacks body and needs a perm and then you figure why not go blond as well and then all your hair falls out. Which was annoying, as I was in the middle of some sensitive negotiations with the hit man.

The hit man liked me and so he suggested a group-hit rate. He wonders can I get them all together. Of course I can. They will all be at the restaurant. I will just tell the expendables that the dinner is one hour earlier at 6:00 P.M. They will be quietly bumped off and removed before the others arrive at 7:00.

The hit man is looking at me intently. I am concerned. I remind him that I am not to be pared from the guest list. He tells me I am beautiful. That I am a beautiful bald woman . . . that he wants to take me to Bhutan where women like me are worshipped. He will also take care of getting my nonrefundable deposit back. What better way for a girl to celebrate the big birthday?

Chapter 4
Why can't a man be more like a Woman?

ADMIT that you KNOW that tone Drives me UP the WALL.

OKAY, I ADMIT it.

see there's that tone..

is NOT. —

Renewing vows for the unmarried

Is marriage so awful that you need a party every five years or so to look forward to? "What is it this year, honey? Is it our paper, aluminum, or bronze anniversary? Oh, we're renewing our vows, isn't six months too soon . . . or perhaps, too late?"

It's so unfair. I want to renew something besides my vehicle sticker. I don't see why we, the unmarried, have to suffer any more than we already do. "Oh, are you married, do you have children? (Well, of course she doesn't, she couldn't have had this career if she had to raise children like I did.) This should be said under your breath, but loud enough for the slacker to hear. "Grandchildren? No, perhaps a big dog? No, only cats, tsk, tsk. How many?"

I call the girlfriends. I say: "Have you thought about renewing any vows?"

"How about celibacy?" Audrey asks. "Didn't you just go to your high school reunion, wasn't that humiliation enough?"

I say this is different; this celebration is going to be on our terms. We get to decide who's a success, what accomplishments we're going to honor. The only thing I insist on is that Kahlil Gibran's *The Prophet* be read at the ceremony, since I didn't get to hear it at my wedding. No one has any good ideas. Bitsy wants to celebrate animals because they love us unconditionally. "Oh, really," I say. "Just try feeding one of them some food they don't like or bringing a surprise guest into the house."

My God I have to do everything! "Okay," I say. "We are going to renew our vows of friendship. Each one of us will write a short essay, a reminiscence of how we met, a haiku poem of rebirth, using spring as the metaphor, and then we all prick our fingers and become blood sisters."

"I want to dress in white, wearing a veil and carrying flowers." That's Bitsy, she never got over missing first communion because her parents were Buddhists at the time. But she has a point. Why not wear white? Isn't that the main reason women get married, the marvelous white gown? It's such a wonderfully wickedly wasteful purchase. . . . Never worn again, available only on the wedding video. Yes, DVDs; everyone will get a copy of the ceremony. The four of us will have a group photo in the *New York Times* and if they refuse to put it in, we'll sue them and get our photograph in that way. I am on a roll now.

"Can we have the ceremony at a hotel?" Audrey wants to know. "Of course," I say, "but let's make sure this party can be distinguished from the ones we've planned for our individual wakes. We don't want to confuse some of our dottier friends." It's agreed and we all arrange to meet in a week to read our poems and look at hotel packages. At our next meeting we will interview bands, trios, and small orchestras. After that it's the caterer and flowers. Sally suddenly announces she wants her own renewal of vows party. I am at first impatient. I say the idea of renewing vows is that you do it with another. She doesn't see why and in the end I give in. She agrees to come to another party later, for the two of us.

In the meantime Bitsy calls. She has talked to her ex-husband and he's agreed to get divorced again, just so they can have a second chance to throw recriminations at each other, including some they hadn't thought of the first time . . . maybe argue over the possessions that one of them appropriated, not because it belonged to them, but to cause the most pain possible.

I think this divorce redux is a good idea, even though I didn't come up with it. I ask Bitsy if all the girlfriends can take part. Can we stand up like we did when she was originally married, but this time dressed in tasteful black sheaths, with bright red lipstick and white flowers in our hair . . . a wedding noir . . . play some Robert Palmer . . . "you like to think that you're immune . . . you're addicted to love . . ." She enthusiastically agrees. Now I have to find a judge/minister, maybe online, maybe an out-of-work actor, who can put together some poetic lines on the subject of divorce, and how it has a sacred aspect.

I am sitting alone in the dark when a lightbulb goes on in my head; the light is so bright that Bitsy calls from downstairs to see what's going on. Audrey comes over having felt the vibrations of my brain waves a mile away. "Gay marriages!" I say. "When they are legal throughout the U.S. there will be a demand for weddings, a boon for wedding planners, and then soon after couples will be looking toward renewing their vows, which means us." "Leave it to you," Audrey says, "to find a way to turn a historic civil rights victory into an opportunity to benefit commercially." "As women age, they become tougher, more like men, and men become more nurturing. It's a fact," I say. "I can't fight it."

As women age, they become more like men, and men become more like women

"As women age," I read, "they become more like men and men become more like women."

"You can't win for losing," I groan. When is that paradisiacal moment when men moderate their tone of voice and women stop saying to men: "You do that all the time," when really it's not more than 80 percent true. When will we reach the blissful moment when women say: "I wish you wouldn't say that so often, honey," and your man says: "I know, I know I do say it too often." It's like the moment before the autumn leaves begin to fall or before the snow-covered peaks turn into an avalanche, covering your quaint Swiss hotel.

Let me say right off the bat that I detest articles about how dog training applies to men as well. I think those strategies are demeaning to both of you. Men, please just give in. Most of us don't want to manipulate you, we just want you to retain your upper body strength and lose the attitude.

I don't want to become more like a man. I don't want to watch sports. I will never want to watch sports. I don't want to hear that the film I'm nuts about is a chick flick. I just want you to appreciate it as much as I do, without demanding that I see a movie where things are blown up by robots. Couldn't you change and I remain the same? Is that too much to ask?

Why can't a man be more like a woman? Where is the man whose eyes light up when he sees that there's a coffee fudge banana split with mocha ice cream on the menu? Does it have to blow up? Can't it just flame up? Let him order the salad . . . I'm having the medium rare, extra large New York rib-eye steak with a side of french fries drenched in salt. And I never want you to use that "tone" with me again and don't ask me what tone, because you know what tone, and finally you will admit that you know that tone rings all my buzzers, pressed my buttons, and you will finally say, "Yes, I was pretending not to know what you meant because I knew it drove you nuts." And I will not have to give in on anything and I can still make fun of you for not seeing your glasses when they are right in front of you and I will not be expected to go to the one place that I know your car keys are because that is not my job. In fact my only job will be to mail things at the post office and go to flea markets and make sure my lingerie is beautiful and folded neatly in the drawers. That's right, I will have all the drawers and all the closet space and you will keep your stuff in a pup tent in the backyard.

Special coupons for your man

These are to be left on his pillow or in his briefcase or taped to the gas tank of his car, as a pleasant surprise and to show him how much you appreciate everything he is.

> I will take your car in to be detailed and pay for it, if you buy me a new car, one of those little bitty BMWs and make it a convertible.

I will put the toilet seat down without comment for a full year, if you walk the dogs and take the animals to the vet in the middle of the night when it's snowing and act as if it's no problem.

I will watch one of the following, showing enthusiasm, but not so much that it seems ironic, on the first Thursday of the month: Japanese anime, a samurai movie with or without animation, a film where buildings, bridges, etc., blow up or where large genetically altered Godzilla-like creatures crush stuff, if you watch whatever I want the rest of the time.

I will not insist that you pick up your stuff. I will pick it up without comment, even smile pleasantly, if I never have to cook another meal again.

I will mow the lawn assiduously if you swear in front of a judge that next year we will put in a pool where the lawn was.

I will not make you renew your wedding vows. If I feel jealous because other couples are doing it, I will let you write your vows on the computer and I will read both parts . . . and you don't have to come to the party either, as long as I can have any size party I want, on any continent. With an open bar.

I will take care of renewing your license plate, ordering any vehicle stickers, and take your car in to have the emission checked if you will learn to swing dance, tango, Lindy Hop, and salsa or if you really don't want to, if you promise to be truly happy for me if I find a younger man who likes to do all that and never bring it up, no matter how provoked you are. You are not allowed to follow suit. Yes, that's just the way it is.

I will buy you a top-of-the-line snowblower, with a built-in satellite computer, or any other bells and whistles, if you clean my car off every time it snows and start it up, so it's warm and cozy when I get in. If we should at any time have a garage, and cleaning off the car is moot, I want one of those indoor lap swimming pools instead.

I will make you coffee in the morning, as long as I don't have to drink it. My coffee is not up to my standards. I will be having coffee out. Thank you, but I prefer to go alone. I need quiet time. I'll bring you back a bagel with cream cheese. You can read the *New York Times* while I'm gone. Please recycle it before I get back. As for myself, I'll be reading a brightly colored tabloid aimed at those with short attention spans who prefer to read about celebrities rather than wars in far-off countries.

Here are things I hate to do: fill up my car with gas and empty the dishwasher. Of course there are other things I hate as well, such as bringing the garbage downstairs. That is a man's job for reasons that I will not go into right now because I don't want to be offensive. I haven't yet thought of what I will do in exchange, but it will come to me. Just hang in there. This may be considered a wild card.

I was watching a documentary about polygamy. The husband admitted that he might need all these wives because his mother had been an alcoholic and he felt insecure and unloved and had to fill the hole in his heart with wives. Or maybe the guy is just amazingly selfish and women are stark raving nuts to put up with this.

The children were interviewed on the subject of multiple marriages. They were amazingly rational. One wished the candidate for third wife would disappear because it would mean he would get more of his father's attention. Whoops. A dad that doesn't give his children enough attention . . . what will they do to fill the hole in their hearts? The two earlier wives veto the candidate. Did I mention they're all blondes, but the new one wears makeup, jewelry, sports a better haircut, and has an advanced degree? The big complaint is that she doesn't pitch in; she's not consumed with chores. She is selfish. She doesn't think of the needs of the family twenty-four hours a day. I think they hate that she is so thin and wears so much jewelry. I felt unusually out of sympathy with her. By the end I felt she wore too much jewelry and I suspected she didn't understand sharing her man.

The husband cannot believe that he can't get what he so clearly deserves, a third wife. When the first wife, usually a saint, says she can't take it anymore, he capitulates. He appears to accept the majority decision.

It's my personal opinion that he is going to end up cheating on the others with the wife they wouldn't let him have. In addition there was a hint, just a hint, that she had brought money with her and that maybe he needed a cash infusion for his lifestyle. He had a very big motorcycle. The first wife said that she wasn't jealous about sharing sex, which took place on a rotating schedule—nothing so human as preference for the way one woman used her tongue could change it—but she was jealous when he showed affection to the other wife.

Yes, I understand that perfectly. I once had a talk with a man about sexual jealousy and he found it unbearable and perhaps unforgivable that his partner could have had sex with another man. This may be a gender difference that is not widely known. Yes, damn it, I discovered it, me, and no one else!

My jealous heart

How are you feeling?

How do you think I feel? I've been in bed for almost two weeks; I feel dizzy every time I try to stand up; I'm coughing my guts out, my nose is stuffed up; I can't sleep because when I lie flat I can't breathe and when I sit up I can breathe but I can't sleep. My hair is dirty, my house is dirty. I'm behind in my work. I'm depressed. How do you think I feel?

I have something to tell you.

Well, tell me. You left me here alone for hours. I'm sick. I'm bored. What kind of a friend leaves a sick person alone for hours. I didn't know where you were. And now you have that voice on you. Now I'm nervous. Tell me what you've got to tell me. Get it over with.

I just slept with Bobby.

You just had sex with my lover downstairs? With me lying here sick as a dog, dying for a cup of tea, my throat so scratchy I'd be happier dead, and meanwhile you're downstairs having sex with Bobby. My best friend and you betrayed me—betrayed me while I had a fever. I can't believe it.

I still like you better than him.

Really . . . ? Well, okay then.

My cat and I are the same age

"No, I'm not kidding." I say. "Buddy is sixty-seven and so am I. I know you think that every cat year is worth seven human years but that's not quite accurate, the formula is more complicated." The girlfriends hold up their hands, fingers forming little crosses, like you do when a vampire approaches you and you want to keep him at bay. "We'll take your word for it," they say. "Buddy and you are the same age."

Bitsy wants me to figure out how old her dog is. I don't know the formula for dog years. So I say, "He's five years younger than you are," and that makes her feel better, because she was getting that worried look and I know she was itching to take him to the vet, even though he has just been there and is in perfect health, because I made her nervous. "Just as people are living longer, cats are living longer too. In fact, the percentage of cats over six years of age has nearly doubled in just over a decade, and shows no sign of stopping." I have lost my audience.

"Cats get senile and they get arthritis, too," I yell at my disappearing friends. "They have hearing loss, their claws get thick and brittle ..." I am happy to see Sally take a quick look at her nails. "They groom themselves less effectively and dental disease is extremely common," I say as I follow them out the door of the restaurant. I am stopped by the mâitre d'. They have left me with the check, again.

As soon as I get home I call Bitsy. Her answering machine is on. I remind her that older cats tend toward obesity and suggest that she and her cat may want to bond by going on a diet together. Then I run down to her apartment and let myself in and erase the message. I find being mean on the phone very satisfying, but as an end in itself.

When I get back to my apartment, I find that my fairy godmother has been there. She's installed a giant sticky wall covering, right near the door. Her note explains that I am to put on my coat and then roll around on the wall until all the cat hair is gone and I look presentable. She will come around and change the wallpaper when it's full of fur.

Pets I never wanted

When I was a child my father brought home a white mouse as a pet for me. The mouse lived in a wooden box filled with Kleenex and covered with a piece of glass, which was left slightly off to the side so he could breathe. I don't remember asking for a pet or wanting one. No one in the neighborhood, which was full of apartments, had a pet . . . we had no television. So I'd never heard of Lassie and as far as liking animals was concerned I had a bad experience with Bambi in a theater. I was running down the aisle (just as I did fifty years later when the duct tape scene came on in *Reservoir Dogs*) after Bambi's mother was shot, when I accidentally crashed into a well-dressed woman and stepped on her spectator pumps. Another scarring experience. She yelled at me and my father yelled at her, which was gratifying. I hadn't ever considered that his hotheadedness might be used to my benefit.

Later I found out that as a child my father had taken home the classroom mouse for the summer. His mother did not approve and the mouse was given to his cousins, who were the only Jews in history who had a dog. I imagine them as the recipients of everyone's cast-off pets. "Bring it over to Hilda's house, she has a dog, she'll take the goldfish . . . what's one more to them?"

My father was trying to relive his mouse experience through me. Poor man, he had no better luck the second time around. My mother hated the mouse and would walk around the apartment bent over as if the creature had aged her. She said she worried that the mouse had slid through the narrow opening between the glass and the box and she would step on it. To be fair to her, this escape scenario had happened many times. He was my only pet until the age of forty.

To celebrate my fortieth birthday, my friend Janice took me to look at a cat that was offered for adoption by a private party. We arrived at a tacky apartment hotel with a good address and were greeted by the strong odor of ammonia and by a formerly beautiful woman. I know this about her because the only photograph on her wall was of her when she was a young model. We were ushered into a tiny living room, with one piece of furniture in it . . . a small elegant couch in shreds. I ignored the signs of what cat ownership could do to furniture. My friend and I agreed that the condition of the apartment was probably due to the eccentricity of the owner.

She brought out two kittens. She put one in my lap and he fell asleep there. I was enchanted. Turns out he had an upper respiratory infection. I named him John. The other kitten resembled a mad woman. I named her Harriet. Janice encouraged me to take both of them because they would keep each other company. I was made to sign many papers agreeing to treat my cats in a respectful way. I remember only one of the conditions: they were to have free rein of the house and no door was ever to be closed to them. I will probably roast in Hell for my disregard of that last commandment. I have added doors to keep them in another part of the house, while I, selfish creature that I am, eat lunch in solitary splendor, without a cat competing for every mouthful.

I keep up the fiction that cats need company. I always have two. Not more than two. More than two marks you as a nutcase. I just learned, in a mystery novel, which is where I get most of my information, that women who have many, many dogs, who cannot stop picking up stray dogs, were probably abused in childhood. I figure having two cats is not particularly revealing. If I had any more, people would begin to have theories about me.

Pets as metaphor

When people see Sally Cookie for the first time, they are stumped. Most cats are beautiful.... Not Sally. After a while, shifting from foot to foot, they say she has beautiful eyes. When I found Sally at the no-kill shelter she had just been returned for inappropriate peeing. The shelter pooh-poohed this, said her owners had acted rashly; she had a small infection, soon cleared up. Well, I suppose you have to lie at a no-kill shelter to make room for new cats. Sally had a marvelously sad story about a narrow escape from death that made her almost irresistible. She was standing on a tall scratching post near the door as I was leaving the shelter and this enabled her to reach out and place her paw gently on my shoulder. I had not found the cat of my dreams at the shelter; the one that would be a replica of Izzy, my handsome, diseased, enormous long-haired tuxedo, with a penchant for opening and slamming shut cabinet doors. . . . I took Sally Cookie, who picked me instead.

Sally's previous owners had signed a form promising they would not declaw her, and that if they did, they could never bring her back to the shelter and if they tried to return her, they would be beaten and have to pay a $500 fine. They took this seriously. Having declawed her and wanting to bring her back because of her issues, they felt they had no alternative but to take Sal to the Anti-Cruelty Society and have her put to sleep.

The Society called the shelter and they took her back, so she was at her post near the door when she seduced me with that paw and whispered in my ear, "I will also sleep on your head, if that's your thing."

Now Sally is truly ill and the possibility of putting her to sleep looms. I have heard people say: "We treat animals with more mercy than we do people. We put them to sleep when all hope is gone." I'm not so sure. If cats had Medicare, I think we would prop them up near the fireplace and have a visiting nurse spoon feed them bottled baby food chicken forever. Incidentally, straight baby food chicken is hard to find. The newest fad is to mix it with arugala or mango or little pasta stars. Cats won't eat that combination. They look at you with disdain when you try to serve it, and then they pretend to cover it with dirt. I was searching for a few bottles of the old recipe in the baby food section of the supermarket—surreptitiously, because I feel I'm depriving someone's human baby of food—along with a woman and a small boy. She looked at me, and recognizing a kindred spirit said: "It's for his sick hamster." Probably we're the only ones still buying the old recipe and we'll find it in fewer and fewer stores. We'll have to recruit an underground cadre of spotters on the alert for the bottles that say: "Chicken in chicken broth." You'll get a call in the middle of the night, or you'll be beeped at the opera. A husky, whiskey-soaked voice on the other end will breathe: "12523 East LaSalle. Ask the doorman for Charlie."

Why not a dog? A dog? Why not a pelican? What are you waiting for?

Now's the time to get an unusual pet. Such a terrific conversation starter. Worth the trouble of training a capuchin monkey to find the remote control. One of my pals has a dog named Molly. He says he's made more friends than he thought possible at dog parks. He has no idea of their names, but he knows the name of everyone's dog.

I would like to have a dog. Small, like a Jack Russell, but with the temperament of some mellower dog, like a cocker spaniel. I can't get a dog . . . the cats would suffer. They do not want a dog, cuteness means nothing to them. I would be indulging myself at their expense. I share my sadness with the girlfriends. Bitsy says she has always wanted a horse and has promised herself that when she retires she will get one. I remind her that we are all going to move to a condo building. She looks so heartbroken that I say we will get a bigger condo, one that has an extra bedroom, for the horse.

I take this opportunity to discuss the staff that we will need to accommodate our new lifestyle. We will have to have a chef in training, someone who is attending culinary school but has not yet graduated; a cleaning service; a masseuse; and now we need someone who is good with horses.

Today I rescued the spice finches from the cage with the zebra finches. The zebras are beautiful but aggressive, and I see that they have pecked all the neck feathers from one of the spices. Now he looks like a woodpecker. Why did I mix the spice finches and the zebras when even a cursory Google tells you that no one can happily share a cage with a zebra? Because a friend who likes to make things made me an enormous and beautiful wooden cage and it seemed a shame to have just two tiny birds that like sitting close together in the corner and leaving all that space unused. I planned to buy more spice finches, but wouldn't you know it I saw the gorgeous zebras and my goose was cooked. Now I must save the spice finches. Even though I have never touched a bird, I put my hand in the cage and amazingly enough I am able to catch one finch at a time and transfer them from the big cage to the small one. I notice that their claws are so long that they get caught on things, like a little piece of string hanging from center of the new cage. Beatrice gets her leg twisted up in it and just swings around and around like she's trying out for Cirque du Soleil. I take her out and cut her nails. I cut Woody's as well. Beatrice bites me. I survive, but not without worrying about avian flu for an hour or so. Now that I have successfully moved the birds from one cage to another, clipped their claws, and been wounded, I start thinking about becoming a vet. Which has become a fabulous money-making career, better than a bounty hunter or arbitrageur. Maybe I can do the course online.

Pets need doctors, too, and they are
never old enough to qualify for Medicare

Sally Cookie has just had a $600 ultrasound to find out if she has a perpetually inflamed liver or something worse. Could someone sedate me and take the big decision about Sally Cookie, the most affectionate cat in America and perhaps the free world, out of my trembling hands?

Chapter 6
Almost true stories of Aging

Hi, PARTS DEPARTMENT?
GOOD, YOU'RE OPEN.
DO YOU HAVE A FRESH
SCIATIC NERVE, A
FEW NON-COMPRESSED
DISKS? GREAT! YOU'VE
GOT MY ADDRESS...
SEND IT NOW... NO,
FEDEX. THANKS.

Please don't upset me

If you can't remember the name of the dessert we had back in 1992 in that dump on the south side, please don't tell me you're having a senior moment. Pretend you've dropped something. Pretend you're choking . . . I will give you the Heimlich maneuver until you can retrieve the memory. I may break a rib, hurry up.

If you have lost your car in the parking lot, please lie. Tell me it's a family tradition.

If you've lost your glasses again, please don't tell me. Insist you were bored with the frames. Never wear one of those cute things around your neck to hold your glasses. Better to lose them than to be inappropriate.

Please don't order decaf in front of me. If you must order decaf because if you drink caffeinated coffee after 4:00 you're up all night, please hand the waitress a note to that effect.

Please don't put your glasses on to read the menu. Ask the waiter what the chef recommends and order it.

If you can't read the small print on your prenup, sign it anyway. Sign it big. What the hell!

All activities that involve keys have a potential for humiliation

Isabelle is ninety-two. Ninety is when you get the big birthday given by your children, and your aged relatives—not as aged as you are—travel from all over to honor you. At ninety-one all your closest relatives are wondering how to get rid of you. Isabelle's purse was stolen. Her car keys were in that purse. She did what all impatient difficult people do who can't wait for someone who said they would get her a new key to deliver on their promise. She's out in the street with a handful of mystery keys she found in the junk drawer and she's trying them in her car door.

A neighbor reports her to her niece. "Your aunt's out in the street, trying every key in her possession to open the car door. She must be barking mad!" I tell her niece that I lost my car the other day because I had gotten a fabulous parking spot in a neighborhood that I drive to all the time. It's where I spend too much money on clothes. I have never before found a fabulous parking spot in that neighborhood and the novelty of it caused me to forget where I parked my car. After walking many blocks in a fruitless effort to locate my piece-of-junk car, I find a very good breakfast restaurant and have a crepe stuffed with Brie and pears. The pears were a bit hard, but I find saturated fat clears my head. I left the restaurant and voilà, there's my car.

Should I start to worry?

I have done it before. Left my key in the front door lock, putting my downstairs neighbors at risk. I decided to attach the key chain with the dinosaur whose mouth lights up to my wallet, figuring that the weight of the wallet plus dinosaur will alert me to the key in the lock. Yesterday I notice that my wallet and etc. are on the hall stairs, put there by my neighbor. Evidently, the key had been in the lock, the wallet had fallen open, and a twenty was sticking out. Should I start to worry?

I seem to lose a lot of glasses. No, I don't remember where I last saw them. What an odd question, but that seems to be everyone's first question. My glasses are very light, so they make no sound when I drop them getting out of the car. They are still quieter when I leave them on a table in a restaurant.

I have to buy yet another pair. Shawn, the manager of my optical boutique, tells me I am now entitled to a special customer discount, probably because I can be counted on to lose my glasses more often than the average woman. I am not counting sunglasses. I know people lose sunglasses often. I don't own any. I squint when it's sunny.

He leans forward and asks me, "Did you lose the glasses that Larry's father fixed for you?" Those were my favorite glasses; the ones that made me look like Jean-Paul Sartre. When one of the nosepieces unexpectedly broke off, I took them in. I was told that because the glasses were all one piece, there was no way to replace the nose guard. I was heartbroken. Larry said, "My dad in Utah can fix these." We sent them to Utah. They came back as good as new. Larry's father had noticed a few scratches and repainted the frames as well.

"Yes," I whisper. "I lost those, too. Please don't tell Larry."

I ask if he will make a printout of every pair of glasses I've purchased at their store. He agrees because I am a good customer. I want to know the worst. Turns out I average a new pair of designer frames every six months. This doesn't seem so bad. I try to pick a new pair of frames in plastic. Plastic is less expensive. They seem ugly compared to the lightweight titanium ones. I can't do it.

Today one of my coffeehouse pals notices my glasses. He finds them fabulous and says: "You would like my mother, she's an optician. She sends me new frames all the time. I must have forty pairs around the house." I start hyperventilating. He offers to have her send me some if I can give him the name of the company and the style number. I blow off work and spend the rest of the day trying to photograph my glasses. Today I will try and locate the designer online and print out the whole fabulous designer line.

The possibility of a bargain in frames does not make me forget my penchant for losing my glasses. Today I am going to call a few jewelers. If a wedding band can be engraved, why not my frames? If there were technology available to wire my frames so that dropping them would set off a siren, I would welcome it. Even though that would cause me embarrassment in restaurants. No, I can't stop eating out. It's one of the indulgences of the aged. I visit a jeweler and ask him about engraving my glasses. He screws up his face as if I have made an improper suggestion and says he uses an engraving machine that only works on round things, like rings. I am crushed.

Find something to be grateful for every day: Kama Sutra for the soul

"You want me to do what with my legs?" I ask my old lover. "I can no longer put my legs in that position." Oh, wow, I was mistaken.

Dating is better when you're older: Dr. Phil for the soul

I go out to dinner with my dancing buddy, I have half a Xanax in my pocket that I can swallow without water and without attracting attention to myself. It turns out not to be necessary. I find that my mother's voice has been stilled. I do not need to ask him more questions than politeness warrants. He asks me questions. They are good ones. He encourages me to order a bowl of mashed potatoes and the macaroni and cheese. He pays the check. I drive myself home and he goes on to take tango lessons. Life is good, but I shouldn't drink coffee after 10:00 P.M.

Better than a personal assistant . . . a fairy godmother who visits on a daily basis

I conjure up a fairy godmother, divine intervention, deus ex machina, someone waiting in the wings to take my life in hand, whose sole mission is to galvanize me into action against my will.

MONDAY: I look up and a rather plump woman wearing a tiara on top of brassy blond hair is humming and hanging up my clothing, stuff that had been draped unattractively over chairs for a week.

She says: "Isn't it more pleasant to open your eyes to a room that's neat and serene?" "Uh-huh," I say. She nudges me. Suddenly I'm standing. She's giving the finches fresh water and feeding the cats. "Get dressed," she says firmly. I look at the clock. It's 6:05. She hands me my favorite pen and my notebook. "Go sit at the coffeehouse," she says. "It's not open yet," I whine. "That's true," she agrees. "You can use the time before seven thirty to write five hundred words in your notebook." And with a wave of her wand and a swish of taffeta, she's gone.

TUESDAY: I hear her before I see her, the swish of taffeta and the sound of sequins dropping on the floor as she cleans the kitty litter. Then I hear the sound of the shower. "I don't take showers, I like baths," I insist. "That's part of your problem," she says, adjusting the temperature. After my shower, which is curiously refreshing, she holds a towel up and gestures for me to step into the bedroom, where my clothes are laid out. My jeans are ironed and have a crease in them, as do my blouse, bra, and underwear. I pick up my notebook and pen. I wonder if I will have to leave the house and sit outside at the café when it's winter.

WEDNESDAY: I feel sequins on my face. I get up. She says, "You can write until nine forty and then it's to Pilates class with Joan Marie." She tells me I am allowed telephone contact with friends after Pilates. In the evening she appears with a beet salad and an artichoke. At 9:00, she brings me my dancing shoes and money for the cover charge and parking at the Green Dolphin. "I don't want you parking on the street, it's too dangerous." She wags a bejeweled finger at me.

THURSDAY: She's doesn't show up. I stay in bed all day.

FRIDAY: I hear the welcome sounds of her stiletto heels and the swish of taffeta. "I was indisposed," she says. She taps my forehead with her wand, removing the two indentations between my brows. "Better than Botox," she says. She's back. I weep with happiness.

SATURDAY: I am lying on the couch, thinking of errands and looking at the trees outside and then up at the ceiling. I am in the perfect position to see all the cobwebs and to think about removing them. I don't stir. Suddenly she is towering over me. "Get up," she says. I moan, but I don't move. "Get up." She begins rocking the couch until it is upside down and I am under it. I scramble to escape. She wipes my face with a moist towel, runs some lipstick over my mouth, hands me my car keys, and rushes me out the door.

SUNDAY: I hate Sundays because it's the day I have to take my weekly Fosamax pill. I have trouble swallowing pills. She lifts me effortlessly out of bed and touches my throat with her wand. "Your throat is open now," she says. "You can swallow any size pill, you could be another Linda Lovelace if you choose, but I don't advise it," and she's gone, having taken two bags of trash with her.

The girlfriends discuss plastic surgery

The girlfriends are talking about plastic surgery. One of us has a friend who knows everything about everything and she is going to find the best surgeon for eye lifts. Yes, she will also look into mini lifts, the kind you can get at 11:00 and be out to lunch at 1:00.

Someone says, "Did you see De Niro on that TV? The man looks like a frog."

"I don't care about De Niro, and believe me, he doesn't care about looking like crap. I am only interested if I hear he suffers from hot flashes and I don't care about eyelids." I bang my fists on the table. The girlfriends go on alert. We are in a restaurant, of course, and I am irritated because there is absolutely nothing I can eat on the menu and I hate the decor and they're afraid I'll ruin the party.

"I want my jawline back!" I shout. They have heard this before. Bitsy puts a gentle hand over mine. I hate that. I push it off. "I want my Audrey Hepburn jawline back, the one I had in my wedding photo. The photo I always carry on me for its educational and magical properties." I shove it across the table. In it, I look oddly unhappy for a bride. A young, pretty girl with pearls in her upswept hair, wearing a lovely two-piece Irish linen dress, beige with delicate embroidery, also in beige, on the front.

I look like my mother has taken me aside to say, "It's not too late to change your mind." As if. She doesn't mean it. She fears the guilt that comes in the night. She's covering herself, in case I should blame her for this doomed marriage. Of course I blame her, but not for my marriage, for my life.

"I want that jawline back." Sally begins to cry softly. "I want my thick wavy hair back," she says. We all know Sally has never had more than three hairs on her head, none of them wavy, but okay, we say, there's a stylist out there that can put a wave in your scalp—whoops!—hair. And then Bitsy calls out for the washboard abs of a preteen and the butt of a sixteen-year-old and, what the hell, longer legs.

I gather the girlfriends close to me. We hold hands and wipe our tears on the soft cloth napkins while I tell them their favorite story, the story of that woman, the plastic surgeon's delight, who remade herself section by section in the image of Barbie and now has a radio show in England and total happiness and we toast her and her tiny waist and tiny arched feet with the product of another magnificent woman . . . the widow Clicquot.

In the reverent silence after the toast, I say: "Did you know that Olivia Goldsmith, the woman who wrote that wonderful book *The First Wives Club,* died during an operation for a chin tuck?" The girlfriends place their hands over their ears and give me the cold shoulder for the rest of the night.

As I get into the cab, alone—no one will ride with me—I lean out the window and say: "Totie Fields, remember her? Wonderful comedienne, died at age forty-eight, because even though she had diabetes and had to have her leg amputated and was overweight, she wanted to have a face lift and died as a result of the plastic surgery complications." The girlfriends don't talk to me for a week.

In our tiny brains, the ones that reach out for donuts and glittery things, the place where the worst part of our mother lives on, nothing counts but beauty. Funny women must have plastic surgery to be pretty or else they feel, what? Demeaned? Vulnerable? Joan Rivers, Phyllis Diller, Kathy Griffin. I am sure my mother would have preferred to see me on the cover of *Vogue,* rather than beneath the fold on the comic pages. Did Madeleine Albright's mother want her to be cute as well as brilliant? Does cute Katie Couric long to be elegant Diane Sawyer? Why does Diane Sawyer look eternally young? Is it Satan or a regime of subtle surgery and dermatological intervention?

On my gosh, I forgot about breasts! How could I? Why do men apologize when they utter a four-letter word in your presence and feel perfectly comfortable in saying: "I'm leaving a big tip for the waitress and one for her breasts." Aren't they embarrassed about their obsession with breasts? I mean, it all goes back to babies sucking at their mother's breasts. It's so immature. How did men get away with turning it into a sexual fetish? Why don't they care whether a breast is large naturally or whether it's been surgically enhanced? Shouldn't women do them a favor and just giggle when they comment on breast size? Shouldn't there be songs written about the silliness of this breast fixation? Shouldn't we sue the men who made us feel we had to stuff our bras with Kleenex? Yet, I was happy when my old lover looked with pleased surprise at my large breasts and said: "When did that happen?" I felt as proud as if I had done something to make it happen, something to please him . . . a nice surprise that I cooked up.

That's my next research project. Asking men about breasts. I will start with the guy who was giving two tips, one for the waitress and one for her secondary sexual characteristics.

Someone to be grateful for every day: Helen Thomas has been making presidents uncomfortable since Reagan

I go to a historic event. Helen Thomas, the reporter who has made nine presidents cringe with her questions and who has a phenomenal memory, is speaking at a luncheon. I am ashamed to admit that I spend much of the time asking a man I know his opinion on my question of the day: "What is it with men and breasts?" He says reasonably that when boys are in puberty and noticing girls for the first time, they see that they have breasts. They become obsessed with them and that's it. I heard this same explanation on an episode of *Law & Order*. Two unimpeachable sources. I accept it, provisionally.

I ask a somewhat younger male friend. He acknowledges that the obsession exists but he says: "I have no idea why." Then he asks, "Have you ever visited the porno sites that deal with breast size? Some men like little ones, and then there's . . ." He searches his brain to no avail. He can't remember the name of the site where women have extremely large areolas. No matter. I am not going on a porno site to increase my knowledge. This is why I didn't become a great scientist or anthologist. Small attention span. Hamsterlike, in fact.

The girlfriends get thonged

We girlfriends are having a riotous good time. We've left our friends behind in the cold Midwest with their lips pursed in envy. We're stuffing ourselves with grilled calamari and

Shrimp Louis in a restaurant in Key West, right on the beach, you know the one . . . laughing and interrupting each other at top speed, washing it all down with Veuve Clicquot, damn the expense, when the woman in the thong walks in.

We are struck dumb, stone women who once were flushed and vibrant. We are silent, our throats cut by her perfect abs and a little butt of steel. We remain in our pre-thong positions, paralyzed, the merriment wiped off our faces. Immobilized for all eternity, except that finally one of us sighs.

Then she speaks. "Well, girlfriends," she says, "the bright side is that if we came into this restaurant wearing thongs, some fool from management would refuse to seat us and then we could hire a lawyer and sue them for everything they have. This restaurant and that big Audubon print over the bar could be ours!" "Amen!" We solemnly drink to the fantasy of our potential to be someone's worst nightmare.

Coming to terms with getting tired of <u>Law & Order</u>

I thought I would never get tired of hearing the opening of *Law & Order:* "In the criminal justice system there are two separate but equal branches, something, something, these are their stories." *Special Victims* is unpleasant, and *Criminal Intent* is interesting only because of the hope that someone will reduce Vincent D'Onofrio to a quivering mass of insecurity. Long ago I got tired of Jessica Fletcher. I was a dedicated watcher of *CSI,* but no longer. I tune in to hear the theme song and see a wide shot of Las Vegas. I tune in to *CSI: NY* for the same reasons. Don't get me started on David Caruso.

As a child, I loved Chinese food, just plain old Chinese

food like they served in my neighborhood, and then I moved on to Szechuan, and from then on I eschewed Chinese. I keep my current love of Japanese food to myself. It spoils my point. Sally wonders what my point is. "It's a way of dealing with our eventual death," I say. "I see the end of life as a process in which we gradually wean ourselves of the foods and activities that we previously enjoyed. Little by little we become tired of everything we were attached to and then we are ready to die, peaceful, accepting, and with a feeling of completion."

"When will you begin to get tired of French shoes?" Bitsy asks. "I think that will be very near my last breath," I say. In fact I perk right up and look fifteen years younger just at the sound of the words: *French shoes.*

Computer as metaphor

Today my neighbor came upstairs to help me with my recalcitrant e-mail. I have been scanning my cartoons weekly and sending them to my editor by e-mail for a year. Suddenly my computer absolutely refuses to send the scan. I try over and over again, reducing it, sending it to my editor's other mailbox, desperately trying to fool the computer into doing what it's always done. I hesitate to call Tom unless it's a real emergency. He's known me too long. He always starts off badly by asking me: "What did you do?" The other day I remembered that in the past I have taken a problem into my own hands and not called anyone until I ruined the printer by putting WD-40 on the carriage. Tom insists I put butter on it, but that is ridiculous.

Finally I throw in the towel and ask him to take a look. It's always fascinating to watch a man at work. He looks up past e-mails to my editor to see how successful e-mails were sent. That would never occur to me, nor would checking every setting that might have some influence on my attachment. I never knew that one could select whether e-mails came in automatically, one a minute, one every five minutes, every week, or could be asked for manually. He puts it on manual. I hate it. I am addicted to the surprise of receiving e-mails out of nowhere in their delicious bolder type, announced with a sound effect.

I serve Tom coffee. I clean up various piles of trash. I put in a load of laundry. I lie on the couch and look at the trees. Finally Tom asks, "How old is your computer?" "It's six years old." "Six is very old for a computer," Tom says solemnly. (I'm wondering what the equivalent is in man-years. I can hear Mel Brooks doing his two-thousand-year-old-man routine. I'm sure my computer is not that old.) He continues, "See how it's trying to send the file? Hear how it's struggling?" And then it suddenly stops. "It's like it's connected and suddenly it loses the signal. You can't ask it to do too much. It freaks out. Look, after all this time it's only managed to send ten percent of the scan."

Tom restarts the computer, hoping it will experience a second wind. "That was a mistake," he says sadly. "Now it is really freaking out." He goes downstairs because he can't stand to witness my asthmatic computer trying its best to do what it did so effortlessly in its youth. "Part of the difficulty," he says on his way down the stairs, "is that Steve [our computer guy] stuffed too much RAM into an old system and it just can't handle it . . ." I hear Jack Nicholson: "You can't handle the truth!" Evidently this is the case for computers too. By the time Tom returns, the computer has stopped trying. . . . I hear it, its tiny voice saying, "I can't, I can't, and please close my window! Don't expose me to the callous glances of the young."

Is my computer a metaphor for getting old? You can put in new parts, but the basic structure cannot hold. At first the body is elated: "Oh, a new knee, oh, swell! I can play tennis just like I used to. Oh, crap, there goes my rotator cuff and the doctor is being mean to me, he tells me I can't have a new cuff and a new hip and plastic surgery as well. Why not! If sixty is the new forty, why can't I have a taut body to go with my taut abdomen, surely we can find some third-world donors willing to supply an entirely new skeletal-muscular system!"

Okay, enough of that. I am going to buy a new computer. Bury my old one next to my cat Izzy and the dead bird, which has probably been in the freezer long enough. There will be a heavy price to pay for a new computer. The learning curve will be onerous. I have bought and given away many couches. They weren't old. My cats had destroyed them or I had merely become tired of them. The pleasure of shopping for a new one and rearranging my other furniture to accommodate it is a delightful experience. One I could repeat every month. There is nothing fun about a new computer.

On the other hand I still have my very old car, which cannot be locked because of some eccentricity in the electrical system. I still have a gigantic boom box, twenty years old, which did not come with a CD player and now its tape player has developed a taste for tapes. It has eaten Joe Cocker. I can live with it. I have repaired my cat Buddy many times. I will do whatever necessary to keep him going. Please do the same for me.

Addendum: I e-mailed Steve, the computer guy. His view of the situation is less catastrophic than Tom's. It's like the difference between fundamentalists and anyone else. He says, "It just needs more memory and a backup something or other." The whole deal will be $150 . . . $400 with installation. I wonder if I get a rebate for the time he pets Sally Cookie and stares into space. But $400 is a bargain if it means one can replace parts and keep going . . . at least for a little while.

Chapter 7

Lonely

The girlfriends have an emergency meeting

I call an extraordinary and unscheduled meeting of the girl-friends. It takes twenty phone calls and a lot of wheedling to get them over to my house. I have to promise to make them my new strawberry tiramisu recipe. I add details to make my fictitious dessert more enticing. I say it's dusted with chocolate and hazelnuts. Long ago my friends agreed to the fiction that I bake. They show up looking game, but wary.

I tell them I'm lonely. I'm talking about real loneliness. The kind where there's nothing to watch on television, even though you have two hundred channels and TiVo. And you've bought three books, all of which you have already read but picked up thinking they were brand-new even though the author has been long dead, because they change the covers when they go into mass distribution, and although you can still remember authors, you no longer remember titles.

Every book promises to be well-written, thoroughly researched, and guaranteed to keep you on the edge of your seat until the last page. Last week, I left my book in a neighborhood restaurant and by 5:00 they had hung it on my door. If I was married, would I be having lunch out, reading during my meal, ordering a turkey burger, no bread, no cheese, no fries, with grilled onions and mushrooms? I doubt it. I understand how lucky I am but . . .

There is a moment in every evening when a horrid feeling of loneliness overtakes me and although I know that life is a trade-off and that I have traded a husband for the ability to redecorate my house every two weeks, to run off on vacation to places that interest me without having to consult anyone and that I never have to go to social evenings just because my spouse needs support and I never have to watch boy movies unless I really want to, there is still that moment when I fear I have made a bad choice in life and one that is irreparable. I am lonely. . . .

The girlfriends arrive. I tell them I am lonely. "Not again!" they chorus. I wave the tiramisu in front of them and they calm down.

Sally says, "You know that life is a trade-off?" I cuff her behind the ear. She continues, "You could have a demanding husband who thinks that you should occasionally cook him a dinner or bear him a child. One who has told you the same story hundreds of times, which is okay when you're alone because you can leave the room, but when this same story is told in company, you have to look interested?"

"I'm lonely. I'm depressed and lonely," I whine. Sally says brightly, as if she hasn't suggested this many times, "How about mentoring a child?" "The last child I mentored was so brilliant that people competed with each other to mentor her. She became annoyed and told me that she had enough adult friends already. She is the only kind of child I would be interested in mentoring."

Bitsy suggests I work with the truly old and destitute, people who have to decide on a daily basis between eating and medication, and cheer them up. We glare at her. "Or you could start a business like an old-fashioned penny candy store or a noodle shop. You could learn a new skill," she says brightly. "Like identity theft?" I say testily. She is undeterred: "You could be a crossing guard." I interrupt. "Blah blah blah," I say. "Come up with something new or I will do something drastic."

"You've already decided to do something drastic, haven't you?" guesses Sally, shrewdly. "You've decided to become an actress. May I remind you that there are few parts for genuinely talented women of a certain age, and you've only played one role in your life and that for a total of two weeks? Think of how long a real play lasts. Think of your short attention span." I don't hear the last part because I have wandered off to polish the chrome on my stove.

They follow me into the kitchen. "Make us coffee," they say. I smile. "No, no," says Bitsy. "I will make the coffee." She opens the cupboard. "You have nice cups," she says. "Do you have real milk?" I open the refrigerator and bend down to locate the half-and-half that I have hidden behind the calcium supplement in case the diet police visit me, and I put it into a beautiful pitcher.

"Okay," Bitsy says. "Lay it on us. What have you decided to do to mitigate your loneliness?" I take them to the back room, which I have redone. It's very neat and has a nice smell because I don't let the cats in there. In fact I never go in there. The bed is made with freshly ironed sheets, there are two living plants, and I have washed the stickiness off the phone.

"I'm opening a bed and breakfast," I announce proudly.

"Aren't you afraid of serial killers?" Bitsy asks pleasantly.

"Aren't you afraid that you open your eyes one morning and your guest is wearing one of your blouses and sitting on your bed staring at you?"

"You see too many movies called something like *Single White Female.* I only take women who are coming into town to do advanced training in Pilates."

"That only means they could be psychos in great shape," Sally says.

"And breakfast? You're supposed to make them breakfast. Your refrigerator looks like a museum. What would you offer them for breakfast?"

"They seem to bring their own food, all of them are on a healthy diet, and they even leave nine-grain bread in the re-frigerator for me, and then I throw it away." I smile and fold my arms.

"I want to do it too," says Sally. "Me too," Bitsy says.

"Good!" I bring out the contract. I'm giving a course in B and B. Only $500 for friends.

"No wonder you're lonely," they chorus.

Unexpected visits from fairy godmothers

My F.G. makes an unscheduled visit. "I noticed you were low on clumpable, multi-cat kitty litter last time I was here," she says. "There's an all-night market on Damen Avenue. Should I pick some up?" I look at the clock. It's 3:00 A.M. "Sure," I say. "I like the kind in the plastic containers with the screw-off tops." "Yeah," she says. "Like I didn't know that."

"Look," she says, "as long as I'm here, why don't I put some makeup on you. A little pencil, a little eyeliner, some blush and a pair of earrings. Making up at night saves you a great deal of time in the morning," she says. "In fact, if you had permanent eyebrows, eyeliner, and lipstick tattooed on, you would save oodles of time." "What if I just slept in my clothes?" I ask. She gives me a slight slap . . . that woman can detect irony a mile away.

"I know that you have trouble getting up in the morning, so I thought I might send a cute guy over in the morning with a latte and half a sweet roll to help you start your day." "Oh," I say, "well, that'll help me to remember to put makeup on before I go to sleep."

"Listen, since you're being so thoughtful I have an idea I'd like to talk to you about . . ."

"Yeah," she says, "I know. You're thinking you'd be willing to take a chance on love again, but you don't want to experience the pain of loss should the affair go badly, as you're quite sure it will."

"What do you think of my six-month coma as a way of getting over a broken heart?" I ask.

"The fairy scientists are working on it," she says. "Tootle-loo." With a wave of her hand and a flurry of sequins, she disappears.

Chapter 8 Return to Lust

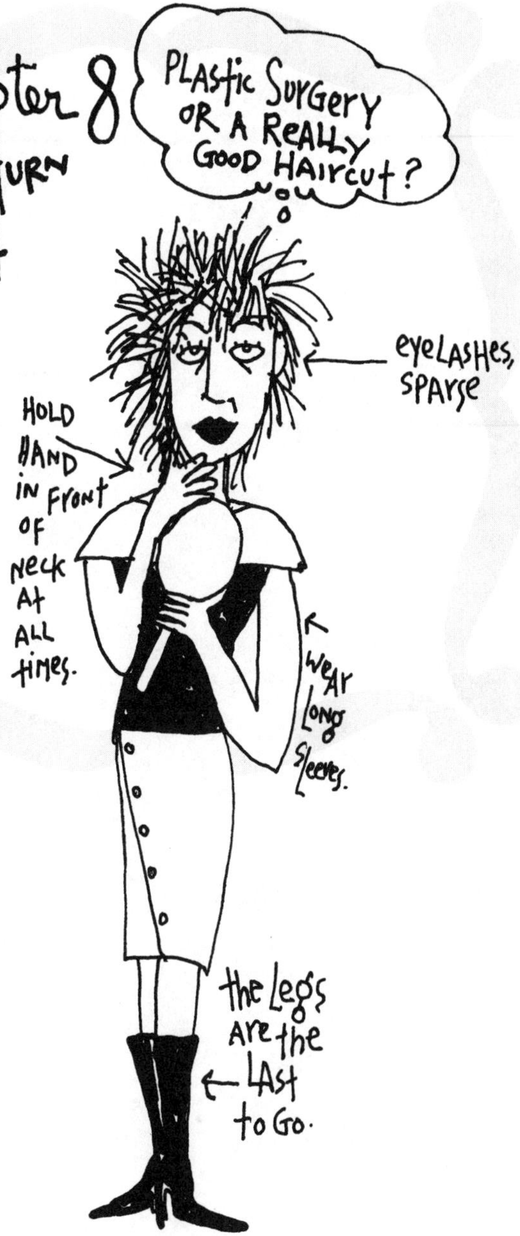

Return to lust

I'm getting myself in the mood by listening to songs from James Bond. "Nobody does it better, makes me feel sad for the rest. Nobody does it half as good as you. Baby, you're the best. . . ." Okay, I'm so stoked I can hardly walk.

I calculated I hadn't had sex for ten years. Turns out that it's been fourteen. I know that because I called Dominick, long distance, the last man I had sex with. I ask him, "When's the last time I had sex?" He's not surprised by my call. "We were together from 1980 to 1989, so it's been fourteen years." "Fourteen years! Are you sure?" I can't believe it.

I call someone who's my age and who I'm sure has been having sex. "Carol," I say, "you're postmenopausal. Got any tips for me, because I'm going to have sex in the next ten days." Carol says, "You think I'm having sex? You must be nuts. I'm not having sex. But let me get a cigarette, because if you're having sex, I want to hear about it." She has no advice, not even about having an affair with a married man, a subject she knows a great deal about. She says, "I have no advice for you."

I'm going to be having sex in ten days. Just from thinking about it, I develop a lump in my vulva. For all I know it's my labia . . . it's been so long. I'm between gynecologists, so I go to my old gynecologist, who is no longer covered under my new insurance. I have to pay cash for this visit. This sex had better be over-the-top.

He's got a kid intern with him. They're both going to look at my vulva, which they have drawn a diagram of on a little piece of paper to protect my modesty (just like the doctors did in China for upper-class women in olden days). He asks me to indicate the area of discomfort. I am almost beside myself with impatience. It turns out I have a blocked gland. I tell him I am going to have sex after fourteen years. He gives me a high five, asks me when this is going to happen, and gives me medication to knock out the infection so I will be in tip-top shape for my rendezvous. I find men of any age terribly pleased and excited when they hear women of any age are having sex after a long time. It renews their faith.

I call my sister, Jana, who has a lot of sex and who expresses surprise that I am even interested in sex. "I didn't think you were interested in sex," she says. I say, "I don't have much time to get my vagina in condition and I can't waste it raking over the past." She says that she always hoped we would have a discussion like this, where she knows everything and I am a pathetic novice. She brings over some estrogen cream, but she has somehow lost the applicator. There are no problems for my sister. She has a corporate job. She says to go to the drugstore and just buy an applicator. The pharmacist says, "You can't just buy an applicator. Are you crazy?" or something like that, in pharmacist language. "Okay," I say, "give me the cheapest product you have that comes with an applicator." That turns out to be something for yeast infections. Yes, I remember yeast infections. I throw the stuff away and keep the applicators.

I call a dear friend, who has always experienced pain in sex until she met her Tantric master and he ordered her a best friend, the BMW of vibrators. It gets warm, I don't know how. I hope it's not dangerous. Anyway, she starts telling me about a product that you put in your vaginal tract, called something like Silken Secret, and her voice gets all soft and dreamy when she talks about it, and she's sending it immediately by FedEx. There's another product she suggests that I have to order online that has a Greek spiritual kind of name, which I order, and then there's Astroglide, for my man. I have always been a kind of disorganized person who jumps into things. I like to start painting the living room when I am wearing a velvet jacket, but this time I decide I'm going to be methodical and prepare my body in a disciplined way for what I hope will be Olympic-style events.

I find my ancient vibrator and carefully remove the batteries because I'm going to put it inside my body and I don't want to electrocute myself before I have sex for the first time in fourteen years. I put the Silken Dream lubricant inside first. It burns terribly. I run screaming to the tub and spray it out. Okay, there's always a glitch. I'm sure Madame Curie had her setbacks. I try a cream that's called something like Euthanasia and the estrogen stuff and then I insert the plastic penis-shaped vibrator. It's very painful. I call my sister. I am angry at her, she should have anticipated this. She reminds me that penises are more flexible than plastic penis-shaped vibrators. I revisit my gynecologist. He tells me I am good to go and I get on the plane.

After I come back, I tell everyone who will listen that I have just had the best sex of my life. One old lover doesn't look chagrined enough, so I repeat it every time I see him. Finally, he says, "I heard you the first time. I am trying not to take it personally . . ." which seems a shame, because if you've just had great sex, what's better than making an old lover feel bad?

How did my old lover come back into my life? Having become jaded with attending grammar school, high school, undergraduate and graduate reunions, he's decided to track down some old girlfriends. I was not the first one he called. I was somewhat chagrined by this. The first old girlfriend he calls is dead, so he is thrilled when I answer the phone. We talk, we e-mail, we turn each other on. We are unable to wait for his scheduled visit, so we meet in a western town, where everyone is dressed in Nikes and shorts and I am dressed for a trip to Paris.

His wife has given permission for something to happen when he visits me. She says, "I'll understand if something happens when you see each other." Before he leaves she changes her mind and rescinds her permission.

When you are the other woman no one asks you how you feel about anything.

My lover comes to see me anyway, because he said he would and because he has a nonrefundable ticket. He intends to discuss the situation with me the next day. I make this impossible by using techniques I didn't know I knew. He is weak and he sins again.

The next day my lover goes home. His wife asks if he has had sex with "that woman." I have become "that woman." This is strangely thrilling. He says yes. She says that she is worried that I, celibate for fourteen years, have given him an STD and he will pass it on to her.

I am so excited about everything connected with this sexual experience that I go to my gynecologist and have an STD test, just for the thrill of it . . . because if you take an STD test, that means you're having sex.

I imagined that the test involved the delicate pricking of my finger in the manner of Snow White, just one tiny drop of blood. But, in fact, it involves a large needle, enough blood to fill a test tube, and my uncooperative veins, which the nurse characterizes as rollover, tiny . . . and bad. This is not so much fun after all.

Of course I am pronounced STD free, which comes as no surprise to me, or my lover. My lover has also had the test, for which he had to travel sixty miles from home, which makes me smile every time I think of it, so that no one in his one hospital town will know that he has been unfaithful.

I must confess that in the forty-five years between that last time I saw him and the moment he plunked down $9.95 on the Internet and was able to find my address, telephone number, and the average income of my neighbors, I had not thought of him once and now I can't get him out of my mind. I told him that whenever I heard Ahmad Jamal I got a rush. I said I remembered listening to "Perdito" in the car and being enormously aroused. My old lover looked pained. "Don't you remember that I was with you in that car?"

The end of the affair

The affair was over, but I was still choked with lust. I needed to repeat the experience as quickly as possible, but with a more appropriate partner. I looked in the mirror. I saw clearly that I needed to make a few adjustments in my appearance if I wanted to attract a man. My face needed to be buffed and tightened. I didn't want sex enough to go under the knife. My normal self-protection had been weakened, but not destroyed. So I investigated the world of non-ablative surgery.

I have now had every non-ablative dermatological procedure available: Thermage, Restylane, microdermabrasion, Botox. I have paid in pain and money. Pay attention. I did it for you so you wouldn't have to. Believe me when I tell you that there was no difference in my face before and after the treatments. I was annoyed. I wrote to the doctor asking for my money back. He replied, "My dear Miss Hollander, take a hike. We didn't promise you a rose garden. Believe me, we are very careful not to. But if you're fool enough to want to try a little liposuction on those jowls, I'd be more than happy to take your money."

My sister chided me. She said, "Well, a woman with guts who wanted to truly be of service to other women, a true feminist, would have plastic surgery and go out into the land of women and tell them about it."

I'm scared but I make an appointment for a consultation with a petite blond plastic surgeon with pointed black shoes. I show her the photos of me before and after Thermage. She tosses them aside without a glance, but not before saying contemptuously, "Those procedures don't work." I had hoped we would bond; have a few smiles over my foolishness in thinking I could get away without surgery. But we did not bond. Perhaps it was her sartorial perfection compared to my jeans and an old, zippered cotton jacket, stained in many places. (Please, I didn't know it was stained until I got home, but I bet she did.) She asked me to take the jacket off, so that she could take before photos. I slipped it over my head. She snapped, "You can unzip it." That's when I knew we would not be soul sisters. "The zipper is broken," I answered. "It doesn't open." Her eyes said, "Who wears a stained cotton jacket with a broken zipper to a plastic surgery consultation?"

Then she told me that I was too old to have a mini face lift and that as well as having a full face lift, I would, in order to look natural, have to do my eyes and my jowly jaw. She adds that one can now also fix crepy chicken necks with a little cutting and a little stitching and a little shoving of that extra flesh into an itty-bitty incision under the chin. The doctor lets me feel the scar under her chin. She shows me photos of her clients before and after. They are average women like me. They looked terrific. She was good, the blonde doctor.

"You have to lie low for two weeks," she said. "You will leave the office with gauze on your head." "Why?" I asked, leaning forward, my face suddenly taut with fear. "Why, to hide the drains behind your ears," she said pleasantly. "And bring your own dark glasses and your own scarf."

I will now read from the "cleaning of the drains" instruction sheet.

"Drains must be emptied and measured at least three times per day or more often if filled. Pull tab up on drain to allow the

reservoir to expand. The expansion will allow you to see cali-brations. Write down the measurements. Empty tube into pa-per cup. Squeeze reservoir and insert tab. This will restart the vacuum. Measurements need to be added up for each 24-hour period."

Then the tiny iron maiden leaves the room. It's time to discuss money and possible surgical complications. This can be done better by a young nurse, whose innocent voice should take the sting from the ominous words. She reads the treatment agreement that I must initial and then sign.

I will now read excerpts from that treatment agreement.

"I understand that the sealant glue that may be used in my procedure is made from human blood products. I further un-derstand that the selected donors have been tested and that the plasma has been treated with a vapor heat viral inactivation process.

"I understand and accept possible risks and complications that include but are not limited to: bleeding, infection, hema-toma, scarring, skin slough, hair loss, facial weakness, patches of permanent numbness, nerve damage, asymmetry or discol-oration of the skin.

"I understand and accept the possibility of less common complications, including the remote risk of death. I understand that the nerves that control the muscles of facial expression can, on rare occasion, be slow in recovering. And, I further un-derstand that I may experience unsatisfactory results."

. . . And after about ten minutes of thinking hard, which is as long as I can think about anything, I decided to get a really good haircut instead.

I allow my newly awakened desire to cloud my judgment. I am so out of control that I ask friends, not even close friends, to introduce me to older men, men who have just lost their wives. I don't want a divorced man. I don't want ambiguity. . . . A widower or nothing.

A friend calls to say that she had run into the ex-husband of a schoolmate of hers at a funeral. Wow, almost perfect. I sent my wish out to the Universe and it provided. It was not his wife's funeral, but someone's funeral. Close enough.

Would I like her to give him my number? No, I don't want to talk. My talking skills are rusty. I am nervous. I suggest that we communicate by e-mail at first. He agrees after Googling me. (I am fabulous in Google. There are pages of stuff on me, some in foreign languages.) After a few rounds of writing, he tells a Bill Clinton joke, I am deeply offended. He suggests we meet face-to-face rather than ramp up our dislike of each other through the Internet.

I suggest meeting at a restaurant, one that offers a hundred different sakes. Several different sakes can take the edge off any first meeting. I'll be buzzed with the fruit of thousands of years of Japanese civilization. He doesn't want to. He doesn't drink. His parents were alcoholics. Okay, I am flexible. I mention France, where they have spent thousands of years perfecting coffee. I suggest a funky French café with great latte and splendid pastries, but being an easygoing kind of person I say I am open to finding an even funkier café with possibly even better coffee. He replies he drinks only diet root beer. In my whole life I've never met a man who drank only diet root beer.

Second thoughts

I realize that after fourteen years of being perfectly happy with my friends, my antidepressant medication, and a very dependent cat named Sally Cookie, I am not keen to begin a relationship with a person who drinks only diet root beer. I am also put off when he says that a two-person family is better equipped to raise a child than any other combination, and because he would be sure to make demands, as real people often do. I tell him I am sorry, that my fantasy life is so overwhelmingly satisfying, so all-consuming that I have no room in it for a real person. He is gracious. Possibly quite relieved.

Messing around with the French

Meanwhile, I've begun a flirtation with Guy, who I haven't seen in twenty-five years. He lives in France. His letters are delicious, an unexpected aphrodisiac. I am ecstatic, entranced by his outrageous wit and his sexy phrasing. He tells me that I am correct, we are having an affair. I try to remember when I said we were having an affair. I believe I said something like "This is too hot not to cool down." He tells me to have no fear. I am in the hands of an experienced man, a man who has had many affairs. In fact, I am Madame Onze, the eleventh in a long line of what the French refer to as "fiancées"; long-term sex partners (as opposed to a one-night stand); liaisons which do not lead to marriage. I am assigned a number just so I don't get a swelled head.

My affair with Guy doesn't demand plane tickets, incredibly convoluted plans, missed messages and mixed messages. It's virtual. I savor it. He sends me hot letters. I look forward to every letter with obsessive anticipation. If I don't get a letter, I send him one threatening to cut him out of my life.

Guy and I have been writing for a year, three or four letters a week. At the beginning we're both in a sexual daze, but after a while our relationship becomes as full of misunderstandings and petty irritations and as demanding as any normal relationship. Our exciting scenarios have grown old. By the time he announces, without discussing it with me, that he is coming to visit, "Chérie, I will arrive on May 20 at 1600 hours," I feel like I've been in a long marriage and I am looking for an annulment. I am, like, so over the whole thing and not looking forward to having this guy, this hairy stranger (I see him as covered with hair, probably an exaggeration), in my house.

Luckily, he has a heart problem. I receive an e-mail saying he's in the cardiac unit of the hospital. He fainted while watching a movie with a friend. I wonder, "What movie?" He writes, "I suppose it was overexcitement at the prospect of meeting you that made me pass out. I see no other explanation." (He mails me his electrocardiogram. When his doctor asks to see it, he said, "I sent it to a friend in Chicago." She asks, "To a friend of your heart?") Guy wonders what would have happened if, in the midst of *le hot sex,* he passed out or died . . . "Would you have thrown me in the lake, Nikki?" "Oui, Guy, in a heartbeat," I answer. He never does make the visit.

Much later a dear friend calls me. She says, "I ran into a woman who knows Guy. He told her that the two of you had an affair." "Really," I say, intrigued. "You mean the kind of affair with sex and sweat and everything?" She rushes to assure me that she did not believe it, not because of my unassailable moral virtue, but because I would have told her about it immediately. I feel quite pleased. Here I am with a reputation and I didn't have to do a thing. Here is an added benefit of getting old. As a young woman I would have been enraged that some man dared to suggest that we had an affair when we hadn't. Now I just think, "Good, this saves time." This reminds me that once at this same friend's house, a woman I barely know said, "I hear you got married again?" I was excited. "Who to?" I asked. She turned away.

Wind me up, Scotty

You know how it is when you are awakened from a sound sleep? You are befuddled, annoyed. But then, once awake, you can't go back to sleep? And so it is with my interest in men.

Before I know it, I have joined two online dating services and been rejected by a third. I tried to join one called something like BigBrainDating.com which matches people who have gone to the top schools, as ranked by *U.S. News & World Report.* I look at their website, which resembles the cover of a discreet romance novel, and I see that my alma maters, the University of Illinois and Boston University, are not on the list. I can't believe that I'm being discriminated against by an online dating service. I rush off an e-mail to them. I say I'm shocked by the omission of my alma maters. Boston University is just a stone's throw away from Harvard, where my ex-husband earned his PhD. Surely the fact that I was chosen for marriage by a man who later got his PhD from Harvard confers some kind of secondary glow. How about it? I sign it Milly. I'm now Milly for purposes of online dating.

Okay, this is avoidance behavior. The truth is, I am not ready. But, while I am not ready to actually date, I am perfectly delighted to browse and fine-tune my online dating profile.

Match.com profiles are arranged by age. I am betting that no man my age is going to trawl through the profiles of women my age. My cynicism has been born out by the utter silence that has greeted my profile. No. Sorry. I exaggerate. My e-mail informs me breathlessly that I have received a "wink." I check it out. The "wink" comes from a man who has absolutely none of the qualities I listed as important in a man in my date profile. He describes himself as having some college, modestly reports others tell him his best quality is being able to get along with all sorts of people. Also, he values family above all, and, and . . . he likes women who are older than he is. I am creeped out. Fine. There's an upside to my wink. I narrow my desires to a man who dances salsa and swing and has an advanced degree in a hard science. Later a friend sends me a personal ad from a university alumni magazine. It is from a man who loves to dance. I call him. I ask him why he didn't e-mail me. He says he doesn't use the computer. If he wants to talk to a friend he telephones. He is not interested in Google; he lives near the greatest university libraries in the world. He reminds me of the man who only drinks diet root beer.

In my profile section "Books that turn you on," I write at length on why *The Da Vinci Code* is a piece of crap and the person who wrote it shouldn't be encouraged. So, if you haven't bought the book yet, please don't. I easily write more than 1,000 words. They only allow for 250 words on the subject. I am cut off in mid-sentence in my rant.

I discover that I can only muster up 219 words to describe myself and my ideal date to "the community." I am allowed 2,000. I can't do it. I don't want to highlight my finer qualities for the community. It's an invasion of my privacy. I know this is illogical. I realize I want to be loved for the fact that, if you turn me around twice a block away from my house, I can't find my way back home and have to hail a cab.

After, I see the movie *Harold and Kumar Go to White Castle.* I realize that I find doper humor incredibly funny. Now, I'm getting closer to knowing the exact man I want. He must be a combination of Harold and Kumar, but older, the age of Kumar's father. Okay, I'm getting somewhere. Also, I have added to my list of dislikes. My man has to have a substantial nose. I don't like tiny noses on men, or stomachs that start just below the neck.

I had no idea I was so shallow. I discover that what I like most about online dating is writing and editing my profile. My dating service allows me to edit my profile over and over again. But I have to face it—in time, my passion for editing my profile will fade. I will no longer edit and refine it before bed every night, when other women are applying cream to their face and body.

In anticipation of this loss, I have taken steps. I plan to put my own personal ad in some prestigious journal. Big as I want, a quarter page, a half page, 48-point type. "Adorable woman needs to be rescued from her TiVo dependence by witty, flirty, trim, swing-dancing older guy with advanced degree who will drive her wild in bed."

Falling in love, briefly

I melt at a sad life story. I fell in love with a guy once because he was not only abused continually at his Catholic orphanage, but his relatives made him and his sister sleep in a garden shed and cuffed them for asking for a second helping. My God, that's a Dickens story. Do you think I am so transparent that everyone knows my weaknesses at a glance and tailors their life stories for me? To me a man who is witty is the ultimate in desirability. Those men are all taken. Those who were witty in their youth and now are married and no longer make the effort to be witty are also taken. Their wives are stuck with formerly witty men with paunches.

Oh, and you know what else I am a sucker for? Childish hijinks. Tell me that you bought watches at the flea market for a quarter when you were a kid and sold them at bus stops to guys who thought they were buying stolen goods, and that you've had thirty-nine jobs in your lifetime, and that you charged your little friends for painting their bikes and when it rained their bikes ran and when they confronted you, you varnished the bikes, which looked incredible until the humidity went up a notch and the boys became one with their bikes. I am not interested in adult crime. Not even in men who get parking tickets. It's the mythic past I'm into.

The advantage of falling in love with men in coffee shops is that you get over them about the fifth time you hear their stories and you still have a pal and an unsullied friendship. Oh, and it's important that they are married to scary women, women who know where you live. That works for me.

When I was young, before I embraced the concept of falling in love briefly, I fell in love for the long haul. I was the woman singing the Cole Porter song: "Deceive me, desert me . . . I'm yours 'til I die, so in love with you am I . . ." or substitute the lyrics, "Bore me, bore me, abuse and ignore me, I'm yours till I die, so afraid of being alone am I."

Around fifty, I had an epiphany. Since my relationships with men continued long past their sell-by date and my recovery period was attenuated, sometimes taking as long as a decade, I decided to stop it. No more looking for love. I realized that my life span was too short to trawl for Mr. Right. And besides, I had married at twenty-two, divorced at twenty-six. I had done my work. Someone had picked me, once. I decided I could lay back. I felt as if an enormous burden had been lifted.

Once, in Ireland I was guilt-tripped into going horseback riding with a friend. I was outfitted in a jacket and helmet, looking adorable. I was helped onto the horse by the owner of the farm who was toothless, but slim. He looked at me intensely for a moment, imagining me lying broken and bleeding on the ground after being thrown from the horse;

his farm and family sacrificed for a whim; and said, "No, I'm not letting you ride." He then reached for me and dismounted me by holding me tight against him and sliding me down along his body, very slowly to the ground. I fell in love. I see it now as the precursor to my groundbreaking concept of the oh-so-brief, no-exchanges-of-body-fluids affair.

Recently I chatted with a man at the coffeehouse who said apropos of nothing, "Men don't change." Then I told him about swing dancing at the Green Dolphin on Wednesday nights. He said, "Good, I've been looking for something to do at night." I also told him about a friend of mine who married a guy who had, without warning, turned New Age: a man who believed in channeling and alternative healing. He ate weird stuff, stuff that tasted like dirt to her and which he insisted had recuperative properties.

My new friend said, "This is what I mean. Say he promises her he will never eat dirt again. Pretty soon, he's telling her he's going out to pick up women, but really he's in the garage eating dirt." Okay, I'm in love.

To keep young, find something to be surprised and happy about every day: crème brûlée for the soul

When Warren Buffett married his longtime companion, Astrid, an attractive woman of sixty with gray hair, you could have knocked me over with a feather. I had color copies made for all the girlfriends. I plan to put them in fancy frames. Here's something even better. His first wife, Susie, introduced him to Astrid. Susie wanted to live in San Francisco without Warren, but she wanted him to be happy. She felt Astrid could do the job, and it seems to have worked out splendidly.

Surrogate dating

Sometimes I take a break from falling in love briefly to experience dating through another. Not successful dating. People who are actually in love are too busy to do anything except gush . . . most of the time they don't even return your phone calls.

My favorite person to surrogate date with is a childhood friend who comes to town once or twice a year to visit her mother. I take her to lunch to hear about her experiences. I reminisce about her dates. She doesn't even remember the one where the guy shook her hand in the parking lot and said, "Good luck with your weird life." I remember. Or the one man who, upon hearing that she was a single mother, said: "You have ruined your son's life."

She has a new story, a more dramatic tale. She meets a man at a party. He is a CEO of a Fortune 500 company, handsome, witty, and unmarried . . . and everyone agrees he is an amazing find. She is lucky. How could she be this lucky? She goes out with him several times. He loans her a book. She leaves it on the bus. She apologizes. This apology turns out to be not enough. He says she is just like his mother who threw out his comic book collection. She moves rapidly away from him and runs into her house. He follows her and begins berating her and banging his head against the wall. She asks him to leave. After he leaves, she changes her phone number and all the locks, even though he never had a key. I say this story is a bit too intense for me. I want her to repeat the one about the widower who traveled from another town to meet her, stayed overnight, platonically on his side of the bed, and upon awakening, asked if he could move in with her, and since he didn't know anyone in town, could she introduce him to her friends and perhaps organize his days? She tells me that one again. I feel somewhat better. I admire her decisiveness in turning him down, the quickness of her decision. I am afraid that I would have let him move in and regretted it by the weekend.

Sex in a plane

I call an emergency meeting of the girlfriends. It's the second one in two days. They won't want to come to my house two days in a row. I say I have put out my back and can't move and could they use the key inside the mailbox. And when they come, I am in bed in a satin bed jacket. Bitsy says, "I can see you're all dressed under that bed jacket."

I reach under my mattress and bring out my round-trip ticket to Japan. Sally wonders how I will bear up under the strain of being in an enclosed space for a flight that lasts so long. "It takes fourteen hours to fly to Japan. We had to sedate you when we went to Cleveland. How will you possibly make a trip this long? Are they putting you in a coma? Is that a new perk of business class, it comes with a coma?" I am thinking this is a great idea, but I know that it's not possible given present drug restrictions. I say I am deeply motivated and I will get there by thinking of something wonderful and amazing.

I was recently on a panel discussing shojo manga, Japanese comics created by women for women. In preparation, I had been reading about Japan. I discovered some amazing facts. Although women are second-class citizens in Japan, and in the U.S. feminists have triumphed and we are more than equal and now we have to feel guilty about whether boys are receiving an inferior education and being treated like defective girls, Japan has many more women cartoonists than we do, and quite a few are multimillionaires.

Of course, this is fascinating to me. But the most fascinating fact I discovered is the existence of a market for manga pornography for older women and that the Japanese have no sense of sin associated with sex. Seems that there is no heritage of Puritanism in Japan and their gods regularly fooled around.

"You were on a panel discussing whether shojo manga portends a heightened sense of feminism in Japan and you come back with the information that Japanese gods fooled around? And on the basis of possibly apocryphal information, you've bought a round-trip ticket to Japan, squandering the paltry amount of money you have saved for your retirement, because there are bars in Japan hosted by beautiful young men who are knowledgeable, available, and can be rented?" Audrey asks.

Bitsy says, "It's unseemly in a woman your age." "Unseemly?" I say. "Unseemly would be to run off to Vegas because I've heard Heidi Fleiss is opening a bordello catering to women's needs for a change. But, in fact, there is nothing that will get me near Las Vegas. Seeing it on the opening shots of *CSI* makes me feel that I've been there every Thursday night for years. And, I have no desire to see it in the flesh and/or listen to Wayne Newton, or that thin woman with the big voice." Sally says, "Where would you rather not go, Vegas or Japan?" "It's moot," I say. "I have nonrefundable tickets."

Bitsy wants to know what's the difference between women selling sex and men selling sex. "Morality depends on the buyer," I say. "And a woman who buys her clothing at Wal-Mart, thus supporting a corporation that underpays its workers and deprives their children of health care, has no right to speak of morality." Sally looks as if she might explode. I move out of the way, but she knows I'm right.

"Wait," I say. "I have just thought of a practical application to what might otherwise look to outsiders as an extravagance. You know that organization for older women that is popping up all over small-town America, where women wear red hats and purple clothing and get together for tea cakes and fellowship? I remember, it's called the Red Hat Society.

"I will organize package tours for the Red Hat Societies and take them to Japan where they can have tea, cakes, an educational tour of Kyoto, and sex with young men, all-inclusive."

Bitsy says, "That's the most sensible idea you've ever had. I'm in." And we shake on it.

Inelegant dismounts

And another thing that we do upon the end of an affair or the dissolution of a thirty-year marriage is invest in a gym membership. Many of these places are in storefronts, so that you can see people running in place or lifting weights. Why are they in the window? Why are they so attractive? Because they are young. If they are not exercising frantically trying to distract themselves from the dissolution of a long marriage then it's because they have broken up with their boyfriends and want to meet another at the gym. Jerry Seinfeld met somebody else's wife there and made her his own. Obviously these gyms are not aimed at us. There are lots of things I would do in a storefront window; exercise is not one of them.

When my affair ended, I decided on Pilates as a way to fitness and distraction. It was in vogue, everyone was doing it. I was told that Pilates would strengthen my core, sufficiently vague. I figured my core was somehow in my middle, my gut.

I needed a strong core to deal with Guy. I went to a beautiful loft studio in my neighborhood. I must have beauty when I exercise.

It was going all right . . . meaning that I actually attended the sessions and could achieve a zombielike state while doing the exercises.

Everything was swell until I decided one day that I was tired of being sorta fit and sorta not, while doing an exercise called "Skating," which involves standing with one foot on the bar of the Pilates reformer (a machine that has a lot in common with the instrument used in the Spanish Inquisition and numerous Errol Flynn movies, called the rack). The other foot was on the moving bed of the reformer. I also had a wooden pole behind my back and my knees slightly bent, pushing out with my left leg. At the conclusion of the exercise, which actually is a piece of cake, one is to dismount backwards, one leg at a time. My first leg hit the floor (it's the cleverer one), and the second leg somehow refused to follow. I flipped up into the air and had the pleasure of seeing myself in a full-length mirror as I fractured my wrist. I feel this fracture prevented a future fracture, the one I would certainly have gotten when my ex-brother-in-law taught me to ride a bike. He had taught various mentally challenged people to ride and he was sure he could teach me. I just remembered my high school swimming teacher said the same thing. Both dead wrong.

After I regained the use of my hand somewhat, I received a sweet letter from the owner of the studio offering me twenty free lessons. How could I pass it up? The usual rate for a private lesson was breathtaking. There was always the possibility that I would fracture my other wrist, and then there would be more free lessons.

I took my cue from the baby boomers who have been exercising all their lives (not me, I'm my mother's daughter) and refuse to curtail their activities now just because the warranty on their knees has expired or their rotator cuff has blown for the third time.

Intricate ankle and elbow ailments have stopped them from tennis doubles. They will not stand for it.

Tendonitis, arthritis, bursitis, and stress fractures are the price you pay for that lean look. They do not intend to quietly retire to growing those heritage tomatoes that taste like the real thing or to knitting socks for soldiers. They do not hear "No." They will visit doctor after doctor until someone gives them a fresh hip.

It's the new shopping.

Studies show that at some point in their lives, most women will experience a blip in sexual functioning, such as loss of libido, diminished arousal, or difficulty achieving orgasm.

Usually the problem can be cured by a visit from the sex fairy, who will place a small patch containing testosterone on your abdomen and then step smartly out of the way, before your drives blind you and you mount the sex fairy and the pumpkin she came in on.

I think we have to entertain the idea that women are not monogamous. They like variety as much as the next man, if only men weren't so dangerous. But can women be allowed to be in charge of their own sex lives? The answer is: Are you kidding? Look how badly they've handled driving. Do they even understand what is under the hood? No, they don't. They just get in enormous cars; pick up the dog, the kid, the phone and drive. What makes you think they will be any more responsible with a drug that turns them on? They are more likely to gulp it down, put on a red dress and high heels and wobble into town looking for love in all the wrong places.

Who should be charged with the responsibility for dispensing this dangerous drug? Her husband, if she's lucky enough to be married. If unmarried, a Girl Scout leader or that lady with the small dog that pissed on your carpet should be in charge of keeping her in check.

Unfortunately, Procter & Gamble has withdrawn the drug Intrinsa from consideration by the FDA. There was a little problem with estrogen; you had to use it with the drug. But I am not concerned. This is merely a tiny setback. There is oodles of money in sex drugs for women and the market will provide. What I am concerned about is the lack of imagination shown in naming this drug. "Intrinsa" doesn't do it for me. Viagra, Levitra, Cialis. Hopeless. Where is the promise, the potential . . . the heat in a name like Intrinsa? Attendants are in the aisle with tiny scraps of paper, the kind you write your best thoughts on. Make up a name for our drug.

While you're writing I want to ask you, why is it that men get Viagra and their problems are over, and everything we get offered turns out to have some kind of great flaw and we can't have it, because the side effects are terrifying? I'm sure you've all seen the disclaimer on the ad for one of those male potency drugs: "If you have an erection that lasts more than four hours, please see your doctor." I'd welcome a disclaimer on our sex drug: "If you take this and have great sex and then die of a heart attack, please don't sue us." Well, we're big girls. We can choose how we want to go.

Men are simple creatures, like anemones or coral. Their problem is not with desire, but elevation. Even they admit it. So naturally we, the daughters of Lilith and Eve, possessing a more difficult and subtle sexual arousal pattern, will have to wait a bit for our Viagra. Our needs, our arousals are complicated, or so we're told. Although the sight of Mark Ruffalo licking Meg Ryan in the movie *In the Cut* . . . Oh, you haven't heard of that movie? Why? Don't be stupid. . . . Because it's a turn-on for girls. We don't need porno. Just give us Mark going down on Meg. It turned me on instantly, no waiting.

As I was saying, we're easily distracted. A shaft of light hitting a dust ball can turn us off, or the fact that we've been having sex with the same man for such a long time. Yes, we're complicated and easily bored.

But I am an optimist. I believe that eventually we will get our pleasure drug and we will get it because there is money in it, and money trumps fundamentalism.

Chapter 9: My Coffee is Not up to My Standards

MY FAVORITE KIND OF COFFEE IS the COFFEE THAT SOMEONE ELSE MAKES FOR ME.

Compensations

The girlfriends and I are having coffee at a nearby independently owned café. We all own stock in Starbucks. Often we try to atone in this way. Every morning I announce a tidbit of information that will make us all feel better about getting older.

"Between the ages of forty and sixty, people lose cells in the locus coeruleus, the part of the brain that registers anxiety. That's why we are all so mellow," I say. They snort in disbelief. It's hard to make some people look on the bright side.

To test the weakened state of my locus coeruleus, Sally pours the contents of the syrup jug into her coffee cup, staring at me all the time. I do not rise to the bait. She then delicately lowers her head, like a big-eyed fawn at a woodland pool, and laps up the remaining syrup and waffles from her plate. Bitsy starts tapping her nails on her teeth, playing with a lock of hair, and has dumped the contents of her purse on the table . . . now she's counting her change . . . out loud. I am sorely tempted to bang both their heads together, but my deteriorating locus coeruleus gives me forbearance enough to dash out the door without saying a word. I do not key their cars either. I have no idea whose car that was.

I talk to everyone now. No one is safe from my insatiable curiosity, it has come over me like a virus. I must chat. I'm doing primary research on aging, not from books . . . from still-breathing sources.

You know how people lament that they have outlived their friends? Len, the bakery guy who delivers at the café, says that his mother, in contrast, says: "I never thought I'd outlive my money."

I see the old guy's T-shirt from down the block. It says, IT'S BETTER THAN BORROWING FROM MY MOTHER. I have no idea what it means and I am not going to ask. On my way back from the café, he calls out: "How you doin'?" "Almost okay," I say. He says: "I'm seventy. After sixty-two, you're livin' on borrowed time." I notice he has no teeth. "All my friends are dead and I don't have any money." He's smoking. At least he's got money for cigarettes. I retort: "You know what the Italians say?" I don't wait for him to guess. "They say 'Even when life is bad it's good.'" "I could drop dead on my way to get a cup of coffee," he says. "I think it's better to drop dead after you get the coffee," I respond perkily. That gets a much bigger laugh than it deserves and I am on my way to Pilates without having asked him how old he thinks I am.

Today he wore a T-shirt that said: JUST TRADE. I ask him about it. The front of the shirt says CBT. Chicago Board of Trade. He says he used to work there, but he had an argument with his boss, and guess who won? Later I ask Dennis, the proprietor of MoJoes's, about him. "What's his story?"

Dennis says the guy just started coming over, about three weeks ago. He used to hang out at the Laundromat across the street. He rides an old-fashioned bike, you know the kind you have to pedal to get going and then throw your leg over the bar . . . he's very nimble, for someone who has no teeth. Dennis doesn't have the complete story yet; he's taking it slow because he doesn't want to encourage the guy too much. I feel the same way.

Today Dennis tells me that there's a guy who takes a small bag of laundry into the Laundromat across the street every day. He's noticed him because the guy talks to himself constantly, loudly and with gestures. Yesterday he came in for coffee and offered Dennis free tickets to see him at the Goodman Theatre in *King Lear*. He's playing the Duke of Albany. There's a lesson in that for both of us, I suppose.

I was influenced by the radio programs I listened to at my grandmother's house, like *Duffy's Tavern,* which always opened with the phone ringing and then, "Duffy's Tavern, where the elite meet to eat, Duffy ain't here." I don't know why this appealed to me. Maybe I felt soothed by repetition at that age. I don't even know what Just Plain Bill did for a living or what the Bickersons did when they weren't bickering.

One of the many things I still dream of doing is opening a coffeehouse. It's close to owning a tavern, but without the twin handicaps of a tavern: drunks and holdups. It would be my own hangout. It would be called Mabel's. I had a wonderful time as a child at my father's little restaurant. I peeled potatoes, I bused the counter, and I danced to the jukebox after we closed up. I met a man there who illustrated children's books for a living. We who stay at home and illustrate

137

stuff are often found taking long breaks at cafés, looking for a chat and an impressionable child to set on the path of poorly paying creative careers.

Talking to Dennis helps temporarily to cure me of my coffeehouse fantasy. He sits outside, smoking and looking warily at the man who wears the T-shirts with big block letters on the back. He says: "When he leaves, my blood pressure returns to normal." Then he tells me of the weird people who hit on his young girl employees, reducing them to tears by their tenacity. He has had to tell them, "Buy your coffee and drink it outside." I am there when his deliveries are late and customers leave without their donuts, without their spinach-filled croissants or soymilk, and when he rushes out to find lids for their take-out cups. Still, the dream is not dead. Someone could approach me when I am in a weakened state and say: "You look like a frustrated entrepreneur, wanna open a café on a shoestring?"

I have enlisted all the Pilates instructors to listen to conversations in coffeehouses and to report back to me. I would like to hear of any conversation which remotely touches on age, but I am not strict. Joan Marie says: "I got one. I saw this woman at Starbucks this morning; she's got this very cute dog. Every time someone pets the dog and says: 'You are so cute,' she says: 'Me or the dog?' The dog snaps at children. 'Bad dog,' she says, and then when they are out of sight she says: 'You shouldn't snap at children unless they are bad, devil children.' The dog nods." Joan Marie tells me the woman was about forty. Fine, then it's legitimate to include in the book. In the pet store, I heard a woman say, "My dog

has given me more pleasure than any of my three husbands."
She was over forty.

Joan Marie has another one: A mother and daughter, both dressed tartily, were at Starbucks, attracting admiring glances from men and boys. Two young men approach the mother, rather than the daughter, and the spurned daughter barks: "She's forty-six." The good news is that you can still look damn good at forty-six and your own child can be jealous of you. Maybe the moral is to send your young daughters off to boarding school before they learn to hurt your feelings.

Next, I ask my friend who's just bought the kind of donut that they sold at the apple cider stand in her town when she was a child and a mocha with whipped cream, which has flattened out because we have been talking too long, "What is it with men? My doctor is one of the few men who laugh." She says, "Oddly enough, I recently had this discussion with an old lover who says men view conversation as combat and the only reason for laughter is to use it to humiliate someone, to score points. Women use conversation and laughter to become closer."

Two different styles of communication. Different aims. Just as I thought, hopeless. I wonder why it is only possible to get this information from ex-lovers. It would have been useful earlier. Yes, I know I could have read *Men Are from Mars, Women Are from Venus,* but I didn't want to wade through a whole book to have my questions answered, when I could just get the info at the coffee shop.

Something to look forward to every day: Scamalittle

Joan Marie says the newest thing at Starbucks is people asking for a doppio in a sixteen-ounce cup and a cup of ice and then filling the iced espresso with half-and-half from the amenity counter. She pays the full amount for her coffee and yet is not judgmental about those who don't. This recipe for cheating coffeehouses has now made the papers, answering a question that I had: What if you want a hot latte? You take the coffee home or back to your office and zap it. Duh! Making the papers is a sure sign that the practice is on its way out. Every day I look forward to the ingenuity of people in the small ways that brighten my day.

Len and Reilly are reminiscing about the scams of their youth. Len delivered boxes of sweet rolls to workers at break time. Many of them would put the sweet rolls on their tab. The next week he would offer them double or nothing. He came out fine . . . the house always wins. Reilly tells me that when he was young and working at a factory, he would raffle off his paycheck every week. Think of it, for a bit of loose change people had a chance to bring home two paychecks! Everyone is happy. Until the boss gets wise and fires Reilly. . . . Reilly goes to the factory next door and gets a new job.

Doctor, can I put this on my Visa?

Sally is threatening to cut up my Visa card. Bitsy is making a budget for me, with little envelopes for each category of expense. I fear the next step will be a loving confrontation with all my friends and mandatory attendance at a twelve-step program.

"Enough," I shout. "I admit my habit, and I'm not giving it up."

It's a full-blown addiction. I now have to use my credit card every two hours or I get the shakes.

How can I eat, sleep, see a film when I know that I'm losing miles every moment I am not actively spending? Using the phone gets me miles, but not enough bang to the buck. Hotels, car rental, that's chicken feed. The only way the miles really mount up is if you buy big.

Sending your children to a college that accepts credit card payments is good. I would have had children if I could have gotten mileage.

The girlfriends look shocked. Not that they are models for motherhood, especially those who actually have children. "Oh, don't give me that look. I would have loved them. I would have been a good mother. They would have been chock-full of self-esteem and self-reliance, apple-cheeked and fun-loving."

They would have been driving early, in their own cars.

143

Each would have spoken at least two languages besides their mother tongue, unlike most Americans, who are utterly worthless in other countries and walk around looking shell-shocked. My children, in contrast, would have been chatting effortlessly, and would end up marrying someone from the Swedish royal family.

My kids would have been computer literate because computers are another nice big item that you can charge and of course computers have to be continually upgraded. And then there are cell phones and wireless phones that are also computers; one can't shame their children by making them walk around with outdated technology.

And then, since my adorable offspring would be multilingual and pleasant to be around even in the throes of adolescence, I would be taking them on long trips, trips where you could see and even buy large, exotic animals, saving them from conscienceless poachers.

You frown, thinking I would put a zebra in an apartment. Don't be stupid. I would have built something splendid for those animals, where they would be free to roam, though not to disturb the neighbors. Loving attendants would kiss and care for them and teach them the human alphabet. I bet I could have bought one of those big old manors in England from a duke who was strapped for cash to pay taxes. A word to the wise; we would all pay our taxes happily, eschewing all questionable deductions, if the IRS issued their own credit cards.

But all this is water under the bridge. I didn't have children. So if I'm having a heart attack and you see a smile on my face, you know I'm thinking about the miles.

Make yourself happy by doing something nice for someone else

Hymenoplasty can be a nice surprise for a husband or a good friend. Prices for the repair of this all-important membrane range from $1,800 to $5,000. "Really, it's not like a heart transplant . . . it's a very simple procedure."

Basic needs: food, shelter, and storage

We are talking about money. I say, "I'm going to have to work until I'm a hundred and five because of all the money I lost in the stock market when tech stocks turned belly-up. Money for the small luxuries that make life bearable." Bitsy mutters something under her breath that sounds like, "You never had any money in the stock market, you spent it all on shoes." I try to ignore her. At this moment I can't remember where we met or why we're still friends.

"Small luxuries?" she continues. "Like that seven-thousand-dollar storage unit from Italy that you had to have last week?"

"I got over it," I say defensively.

"Oh, really? Didn't you give the designer your name, address, and fax number when she offered to do a little sketch for you?" "Well, she had an accent," I say, "and that made it seem sure that she understood my storage needs because, as you know, Americans have closets, but Europeans understand storage."

I felt the need to explain myself to my friends. "Up until a year ago I was a compulsive buyer of art."

"Yes, we know of your heroic struggle with your obsession," they say in chorus.

"So last week I made a little trip to the gallery section in town, just to test the strength of my resolve."

I took the train, saving money on parking, and I ate lunch at home. I started with the gallery conveniently located down the stairs from the El platform.

Would I be tempted by a small precise painting of a bald-headed man seen from above looking at an open book, which could have been painted in 1700 by a Flemish artist, but was actually painted by a student from the Art Institute? No, I was not. "You're very strong," Sally says. I look over to see if she intends to be ironic. She looks innocent, a quality that has been of tremendous help all her life. I met her in college. We would often trot Sally and her huge innocent eyes out when the housemother accused us of something. Sometimes she was asleep. We propped open her eyes.

I resumed, "Nor was I tempted by the Helen Levitt photograph of a bunch of small ragamuffin boys on a New York street in the thirties, one of them on a tricycle, set off by a large empty mirror frame while in the foreground another boy picks up shards of mirror from the gutter."

I wasn't tempted, but I did note the price of the photograph: $3,000.

I left the gallery and suddenly found myself crossing the street, drawn by the magnetism of that store with a French name that means "luminous," and the sight of an extraordinary storage unit with rotating aluminum panels in the window. I entered. I was reverently testing the folding panels when a designer with a Turkish accent approached me. She selected some catalogs and we began with one mind to look at photographs of German and Italian storage solutions and we fell quiet as you do in the face of genius. So when she asked, "How much can you budget for a unit designed for your space, your needs, and your exquisite sensibility?" I said, "Three thousand dollars."

"What were you wearing?" Bitsy asked. Bitsy's feeling is that a designer only approaches people who look like they still have a nice stock portfolio. "Just my off-white slacks and that dark patterned blouse," I said innocently. "And on your feet?" she said. "Were you wearing the three-hundred-dollar shoes, one of the three pairs you bought when you found out that you didn't have that fast-moving deadly cancer?" "It wasn't the shoes," I say testily. "We had chemistry." The girlfriends take sips of coffee and are mercifully silent.

I knew a Russian call girl. She once confided to me that there wasn't much sex involved with her particular clientele, old Jewish guys. She talked to them, she told them stories, she satisfied them with fairy tales.

I have needs as well.

Sometimes, late at night, I'm visited by a desire to talk about storage, or more precisely to have someone at the other end of the phone talk storage to me. Someone anonymous and intense. I'm willing to pay for this service.

I have a Visa card. Is anybody there?

Time to throw stuff away: high colonics for your apartment

I read once that you should throw away a bag of stuff every week: fifty-two weeks, fifty-two bags. This is terrifically sensible and not really possible. Now is the time to look around with that gimlet eye you are known for and make decisions, what will go, what will stay, triage for your possessions. If you've always hated it, but it was an expensive mistake, give it away. I'm bringing all the books I didn't enjoy to my local café. There are projects that I will never start, but I am queen here and I give myself permission to keep all those beautiful pieces of fabric, velvets and satins that I will make a crazy quilt out of should I wake up one morning and magically know how to sew.

Spending massive amounts of money to celebrate new lovers and escapes from death

It is true that I bought three pairs of expensive shoes when I found out that I didn't have uterine cancer. One pair for my uterus and one for each of my ovaries.

When I had my fling with the old boyfriend, I went to an expensive boutique, so expensive that there is no sign to tell you that you have arrived at your destination. Either you know it's there or too bad for you. I bought three tops. Yes, I believe in the magical properties of three. That must be a vestigial remainder of Catholicism, due to my early childhood exposure to the church. Anyway, two of the tops are practical in a way and the third is white, never a practical color for me. It has very full sleeves, pirate sleeves. I wear it to a French restaurant for a good-bye dinner for my French teacher. I am gesturing. I sweep a glass of red wine up into the air with my ridiculously long sleeves. Someone screams. The wine lands, guided by my karma, on the front of my expensive blouse. Over a period of a week everyone takes a turn trying to remove the stain. Salt, bleach, hard scrubbing. Whatever we try there is still a large shadow of the stain, unfortunately not in the shape of the Virgin Mary because then I could sell it on eBay, but just an ordinary big stain and I end up using the lovely garment as a cleaning rag.

Recently I returned to that restaurant with my old lover and when he passed a morsel of delightfully seasoned saturated fat across the table for me to taste, I got the sauce all over the front of my white blouse. Not the same white blouse.

"Déjà vu, honey." But he had the solution. . . . As soon as you get home prewash the blouse in dish detergent in cold water, then spray it with Shout and put it in the washing machine. It will come out good as new. Of course this only works with blouses that were purchased for $70, not the $250 ones.

A different approach to storage

My sister is moving again. She tells a group of friends, over for Labor Day, that she loves to move. It's a way of seeing the city, putting diversity into her life, making new friends, ones that can be easily discarded when she moves to a new place. One woman gasps. Moving equals temporary insanity to her.

Even the idea of cleaning her office is so overwhelming to

this woman that she's cleaning it in quadrants; my sister's strategy for moving is to sell or give all her furniture away and start over. She loves to get rid of stuff. You just have to be lucky enough to be there when she wants to get rid of something you've always wanted. I missed the day when she was in the mood to give away her exquisite Tumi backpack and the blue leather chair that was exactly the right size for me; those went to her younger son. I was at her house once when she pressed a very expensive vegetable juicer on a friend of mine. "It was my husband's," she said, putting it into her arms. "Take it. Do you want this ugly painting of a sailboat? No? Okay, out it goes."

My friend Donna tells me about Lee Anne who lives in 350 square feet of space in New York and has one very small closet, which is practically empty. She has achieved this state of minimalism by not letting her clothes run her. If she buys a new outfit, something else has to go. She is always well dressed. Her medicine chest has three items in it. She has a built-in bed, one easy chair, and a table with two chairs in her minute kitchen. She is a goddess; we cannot hope to emulate her, only to venerate her.

Buying cars when you're old

I thought that my 1994 VW Jetta would be my last car, but lately I'm not so sure. In addition to being unable to lock it due to an eccentricity of the electrical system—it interprets locking the car as attempted theft, which causes the alarm system to make that ugly noise and then people within earshot leave unpleasant notes on my windshield—there's a little rubber flap that comes down from nowhere and hits my brake foot and now the car is reluctant to start unless I give it a lot of gas.

I know I can have the electrical system fixed, and my flopping flap, and my sluggish starter, but like every problem with German cars, it'll be a bit more expensive to repair than any other nation's car.

It's like when I thought I'd had my last orgasm and I found out I would have access to a few more. . . . Now I think it's possible this is not my last car, that perhaps there are more cars and more sex in my future than I thought.

The girlfriends stop by the house and find me sitting in the dark remembering my old cars. They join me in the dark. We put on a Cole Porter song and eat cookies. I say, "A 1952 Chevy, first automatic transmission they made, I bought it used in Berkeley for seventy-five dollars. It conked out every time I stopped and I had to fill it with transmission fluid every day. I found this guy at a garage, either he thought I was cute or he hated his boss, he filled my car free every day. He's gone now, so is the gas station."

"You should never go back to your first gas station," Bitsy says solemnly.

"I think I sold it for a profit to some guy who liked to work on cars. Remember when guys liked to spend Saturday under the hood of their cars, looking at the engine? Those guys are gone, too." Sally remembers her car that sported a claw-shaped bumper, due to an earlier accident. Whenever she drove on a narrow street, too close to other cars, she would get hooked to them . . . only amusing in retrospect. We hold hands and discuss the future.

I say my next car will be very small. One of those Mini Coopers, black body, ivory hardtop. A car just big enough for my GPS and four airbags.

If I truly forgo international travel and choose the USA as my holiday spot, I need a car in good shape. And I need, really I'm not kidding, I need a global positioning system. I can't spend my last good years getting lost. I read about someone driving their car into the River Avon in England, even though there were signs saying, "Stop, you cannot ford here," because their GPS told them to, but those are the hazards of car travel and I'm willing to follow my GPS as blindly as the next guy.

The room is quiet when Bitsy asks, "When can we remember bizarre old boyfriends?"

"Next week," I say. "Bring photos."

Chapter 11
the Bad Food Diet

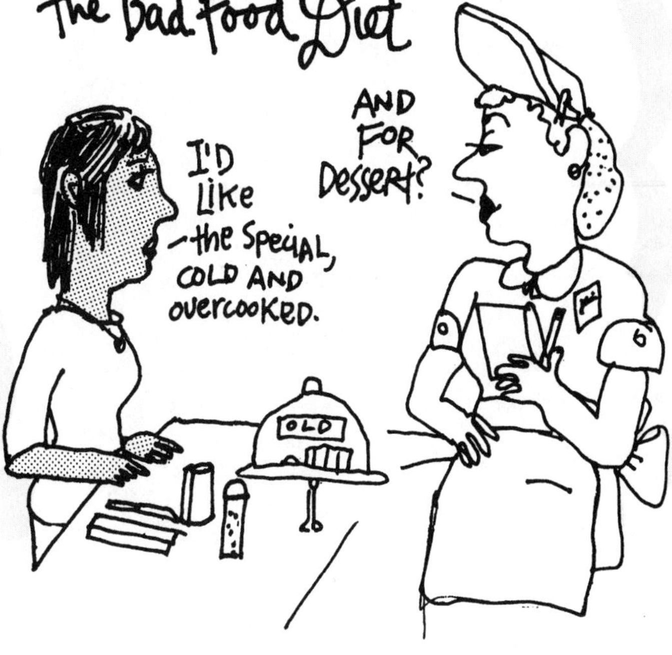

Dieting when you're old

To be frank, I'm short and getting shorter. One of the distinct disadvantages of getting old is shrinking. I have, at great cost, installed a rack, just like they kept for political miscreants in medieval castles, to stretch me. I want to gain just those one or two inches that make up the important distinction between being petite and just short. It didn't work. If I want to look petite, I will have to diet.

Quite by accident I discovered the Bad Food Diet. In a fog of hunger, I wandered blindly into an unknown restaurant far from home, one of those places decorated in various shades of brown: seats, walls, wood. I scanned the menu and prepared myself to eat something I would never eat anywhere else, perhaps meat loaf covered in gravy or shepherd's pie covered in mashed potatoes. It arrives, looking brown. I dig in. The meal is disgusting. I push it away. My appetite is ruined, for the moment; but although the entrée is disappointing. I have inadvertently made a great discovery: the Bad Food Diet.

I have only limited success with this diet. It seems I have an innate instinct for restaurants that serve fine, expensive food. I was forced to turn to another solution. I see a thirty-second TV spot for a diet system. Women shrink in front of my eyes back to their pre-pregnancy size, which turns out to be a two. A two, oh come on! No one's a two. Okay, I suspend disbelief. I order the packaged food (it has a two-year shelf life) online and have a pleasant time discussing substitute entrées with a delightful woman on the phone.

I will not mention the name of the system, because although it worked wonderfully, I really, really didn't like the taste, texture, or amount of the food. But I put up with it and I lost twelve pounds. Remember, I am short. It made an enormous difference. Once someone referred to me as solid looking. No more!

Lately my weight has begun to crawl back up. I weigh myself every day, and when I weigh two pounds more than I think I should, I consider what to eat that day and the next. In a way this is also a bad food diet, because I am encouraged to monitor myself by the thought of the awful food that awaits me should I gain all that weight back.

The Doctor Netflix Diet

There is no need to count calories or move from the couch to the table to benefit from this sensible approach to eating. First you must resist the idea that one needs three meals a day. One or two is enough, if one of them is lunch. Lunch is often an excuse to make up for all the meals you may have missed while in utero or waiting in line at the checkout counter.

Around 7:00 P.M. settle down on the couch with a bag of low-fat popcorn, the kind made without synthetically hardened, hydrogenated oils. This can be made palatable, just as the stuff they pack your breakables in at any mailbox store can, by adding a great deal of salt. Instead of dinner watch one of these movies about food: *Tortilla Soup, Babette's Feast, Big Night, Dinner Rush,* or *Eating Raoul* . . . the latter to be watched only if you are not planning to eat in the near future.

The Hewlett-Packard Digital Camera Diet

A function on this camera can take ten pounds off your subject, and it won't make just your face thin (such an ugly look), you'll be thinner all over, in proportion! Good for men who are planning to lie about everything in their online dating profile and for women who just want to look thinner to attract all those men who are lying about everything.

The Jack Russell Terrier Diet

This diet is only available under special conditions. Say your daughter has a Jack Russell terrier. She has a new job . . . she cannot bring her dog to work and she has temporarily broken up with her love, a self-employed builder who used to carry Fritzi to construction sites in his backpack. Fritzi was never separated from him and as a result she cannot be left alone.

My friend takes in this hyperactive, even for a Jack Russell terrier, dog, and the dog runs her ragged and slim. She drops fifteen pounds while Fritzi is with her. Once the dog goes home she puts all the weight back on. This is the perfect diet if you need to be thin for a special occasion, like a high school reunion.

My sister was thin for both of her weddings, just as I was

oddly dressed for both of them. I recently looked at two wedding photos of her. She is elegantly thin, bathed in soft lighting, gazing shyly at her bouquet. Both times!

Both times I am wearing a strongly patterned dress, red, only my hair changes. I wish I had the dress I wore for her first wedding. I remember shopping with a friend for it and she said, "Don't buy that dress, it looks like a Jackson Pollock painting, you'll never wear it again." She was right, I didn't, but I want it back now.

Casting your cupcakes on the water

Every morning I purchase a white frosted carrot nut cupcake. I used to throw half of it away, but I stopped because I could hear my mother saying, "Children in China don't have white frosted cupcakes. Eat it!" To silence my mother's voice while still controlling my calories, I now cut the cupcake in half and leave half on the counter for others to nibble on while waiting for their coffee order. The other day Dennis, the owner of the café, confided in me that he was eating the other halves. If Dennis turns into a blimp, I will try not to feel guilty.

The "Oh my God, was that tonight?" Diet

I have just combined a can of chicken soup with the remains of the Indian answer to Cream of Wheat, uppuma, which I discovered this morning at my neighborhood vegetarian restaurant, when Janice calls from her car. "I'm outside," she says. "Why?" I ask. "Because we're going to that play at Pegasus Theatre, the one you invited me to this morning, in twenty minutes." I consult the computer. She's correct. I throw on some clothes and leave the soup on the counter. Later, I throw it away.

The "Oh my God, I'm at the wrong hotel for the big twentieth anniversary event and I will miss the food" Diet

I have carelessly let the invitation to the luncheon slip between the seats of my car when I parked it near the CTA station. I decided to take the train to the event to save money. I believe I remember the name of the hotel, but when I get there, I think no, it's not this hotel. It's too upscale. I'm now almost late. I take a cab to the hotel I remember from other events. This luncheon is not being held there. I throw myself on the mercy of Doug, the concierge, and he calls the first hotel I stopped at . . . turns out that's the right hotel. I jump into another cab. I am quite late by now. I run into a woman who is also going to the event. I know her. I tell her how stupid I've been. She says: "That's nothing. I was here yesterday." Why doesn't this make me feel better?

The Everything in Moderation Diet

I'm reading lists of actresses that are bulimic, anorexic, and that other eating disorder that I can never remember. After reading the names of these young women, and they are mainly women, I feel terribly sad and I have to have a donut. As I reach for the donut, I remind myself that obesity is dangerous as well. I have half a donut. Yes, I realize this sounds similar to the frosted carrot nut cupcake diet, but trust me, it's way different.

Something to be happy for every day: fitting into tinier and tinier clothes . . . soon you will be wearing doll clothes and Barbie shoes

Manufacturers of women's clothing have responded to the desire of every woman to be petite. By marking slacks size 6, when they are in fact a size 8 or 10, any woman can fit into more elegant, up-to-the-minute styles. Look like a young girl; pierce your navel to match your size 2 low-rise jeans.

Better than any diet, just bring the subject around to your newly improved dress size and see the secret glances of disbelief and envy on the faces of women who were once your friends.

Every day find something to be grateful for: today it's the opportunity for modest self-indulgence

I praise the marketing genius who dreamed up putting six individually wrapped packets of chocolate chip cookies, each containing only a hundred calories, into a box, because it is more convenient to know how many calories I have eaten if I down the whole box, rather than having to guess.

Chapter 12
Disastrous Apparel
Decisions

Prequel to "Confessions of an inappropriate dresser"

Before I could dress myself and give in fully to my inappropriateness, my mother and grandmother were in charge of my clothing choices.

On a lovely spring day when I was six, my grandmother took me downtown to the Fair department store for my first dress. Up till then, my wardrobe consisted mainly of striped overalls, cunningly matched with striped T-shirts.

I had never seen so many dresses in one place before. I was overwhelmed and on the verge of hysteria. Painfully, I narrowed my choices down to two dresses, each wonderful in its own way, and I vacillated from one to the other like a yo-yo. Finally I took a deep breath and picked the more modest one covered with tiny flower sprigs.

My grandmother left the dressing room to hang up the pink, dotted swiss dress with the sweetheart neckline and the three-tiered skirt and the tiny rosebud at the waist. And, as soon as she did, I knew that dress was the dress of my dreams; the one I would need in order to finish college, marry the teaching assistant in my sociology class, divorce him and move to California, and eventually become a syndicated cartoonist. Somehow I communicated this to my grandmother and we ran as one to get the dress back before it was too late. It appeared to be too late. A strange woman was examining the dress in a proprietary way. I held my breath as my grandmother approached her. Bessie was a big woman; she had owned her own dry goods store, she fitted corsets for a living and had a certain field marshal's authority in her bearing. She spoke to the woman in an amazingly neutral tone, considering all that was riding on her mission. "Did you know," she asked, "that the dots on that dress will fall off the minute you wash it?" The woman flung the dress away from herself as you would a snake, and we rushed home with it. I put it on immediately and my grandfather and I danced across the living room, my skirt twirling in graceful arcs until dinnertime.

Confessions of an inappropriate dresser

Just as Monica Lewinsky deliberately let that stained dark blue dress hang in her closet, all of us have made disastrous apparel decisions.

I have made inappropriate clothing choices from the time I could dress myself. I was totally unaware of my condition. I lived in a state of blissful ignorance. I was like Eve before the fall. Like Lilith before God took her out of the lineup.

When I was fourteen, I took the bus home from the beach, hanging on to a strap. I stood all the way, wearing my salmon-colored one-piece bathing suit. I was not wearing a towel around my waist, a T-shirt, or a sundress. My father greeted me with outrage. I had ridden the bus uncovered. Huh? I was mystified. I understood that he was angry, but . . . I couldn't identify with the sin. I was shaken but I remained in paradise. I have remained there all these years, with one or two exceptions.

My uncle took my cousin and me to a downtown theater to see a Gilbert and Sullivan musical. I looked around the theater and noticed that every woman was wearing nylons and pumps with little heels. I was wearing bobby socks and saddle shoes.

Where was my mother, that paragon of properness, when I put on those shoes? Probably asleep at the wheel, just as she was when she forgot to tell me that people, middle-class people, used second sheets between them and their duvets. I couldn't concentrate on anything else. Even in the dark I was aware of my feet and of my wrongness. I have never since felt that same exquisitely painful awareness of myself.

I refused to wear a white dress when I married or to have a religious ceremony. Instead I bought a beige linen two-piece dress for the ceremony. It had delicate embroidery on the front in a matching color. My husband-to-be asked if I could possibly wear the top backwards, so the embroidery was not so noticeable. That was a sign of trouble ahead, but I paid it no mind. After we married, my husband was disturbed by my white scoop-neck sheath dress with a flat collar framing the scoop. It was the flat collar that drove him bananas. He saw no choice but to cut it off. He was also sensitive to the shape of noodles I used in soup. He felt they were wider than they should have been. He couldn't understand why I couldn't understand how much the width of the noodle influenced the flavor of the soup. I am chagrined now that I understand the importance of the proper noodle width and I think he was right. My God, what he had to put up with. Once I used paper plates to serve spaghetti and meatballs to a guest, with expected results.

Unbelievable, but true, I have just heard via e-mail from Robert, the guest to whom I served the spaghetti and meatballs on the soft paper plate. He went on to graduate school and then to the World Bank, spent twenty-two years in Washington, D.C., retired, and now lives in London. He remembers the spaghetti on paper plate incident. He interpreted it as a sign that he was being welcomed into our intimate circle, an honor.

This forces me to call my ex-husband to see how he interprets the incident now that he is old. He can't remember it. He barely remembers Robert. I ask him how he felt about getting old. He has a thick Hungarian accent. He said: I am filled with *dread*. He sounded like Bela Lugosi talking about the sun in the morning. I was immensely cheered up.

Perhaps I do offend others by my clothing choices, as the French are said to be caused acute pain by the sight of a woman in a jogging suit. I have caused pain, I know it . . . left people clutching their stomachs, but I am strangely untouched by it. My clothing mistakes have continued unabated. Why don't I learn? Why don't I suffer more? I wore short shorts to my freshman English class. The professor looked at me intensely and said, "Thank you for wearing those shorts." Bad men have led me astray. . . . That's why.

Once a friend made me a wonderful hand-painted T-shirt. It was oversize and fit me like a dress, except it was shapeless. I noticed that, so I put a belt on it. The closest I could come to matching the colors on the shirt was a brown rubber belt that looked something like the leather ones we wore around our Girl Scout uniforms. I strapped it on.

Then I put on little baby-doll socks. The socks were given

to me by a woman I didn't like, so there was really no excuse for them, except they were also hand-painted.

Finally I slipped on the little Mary Jane–type shoes that my cousin Gail had given me. Cousin Gail, who came back into our lives after she had been ripped, at age two, from the arms of my aunt, the sister of her dead mother, by her father, who came on the midnight train from California, and who we never saw again until she came to visit and bought me those shoes.

My friend Alicia was in town and we were going to an elegant restaurant for lunch. She looked at me and said, "Is that all you're wearing?" I chose to take her literally. It was summer. Of course it was all I was wearing.

What she meant was . . . "What, are you nuts? You're middle-aged and you're wearing an oversize T-shirt with a pair of funny shoes that have been out in the rain and hand-painted socks to a restaurant with a French name? Put on that little black dress."

But women are terrified of directness. We don't want to hurt anyone's feelings. This handicap leads us into long affairs with weird men and the purchase of clothing we later regret. Instead, Alicia looked at me for a moment and said, "You look fine."

I know what she was thinking. "I am not her mother. I have never seen Nicole throw a tantrum, but she could turn petulant and I have a restricted airline ticket—it can't be changed for under five hundred dollars, so this is not the time to find out her true nature, and anyway, Nicole is an artist, or at least a cartoonist. Maybe it's okay for her to look goofy. Or maybe—and this is a horrible thought—what she's wearing is all the rage and I just don't know it because I'm stuck in a small town in Massachusetts where style is a foreign concept, which is totally my ex-husband's fault. I should have been back in California by now."

"No, it's fine," she says, and we go on to Monique's and give every woman there something to be grateful for . . . she's not wearing what I'm wearing.

Chapter 13
Rethinking My Hair

Head in flames

I am rethinking my marvelous white hair. People come up to me on the street and say, "You have wonderful hair." These are the same weird people who ask if they can stroke the bellies of pregnant women. Maybe I should dye it a magenta-ish color, making my head seem to be in flames.

In this, I am like my mother, relying on my hair to provide me with entertainment. I hate that white hair announces that you are old, whereas the entire world agrees to the fiction that dyed black hair says "young" or "still making a valiant effort" or "French."

I'm saving hair coloring for the night I wake up bored at 3:00 A.M. and there's a bottle of burgundy dye calling me from the medicine chest.

The branch doesn't fall far from the tree

My mother's hair was white when she was nineteen, a lovely blank palette enticing her into endless experiments with color. I didn't see her with white hair until I was in my twenties.

Once, due to a miscalculation at the beauty shop, her hair was dyed pale green. As soon as I saw her, I cried and threw myself around the room. At the time, I was at a friend's house and her mother, who was the perfect mother, said,

"Your daughter is upset because she doesn't recognize you as her mother. She thinks her mother is gone." My mother and I were both struck by the truth of that explanation.

What made this woman the perfect mother? She had a dress-up drawer filled with gauzy fabric. She had the same last name as we did. I could have easily changed places with her daughter. She served us canned SpaghettiOs for dinner. Of the many things my mother disapproved of, canned SpaghettiOs topped the list.

Naturally I was always doing something to my hair. My earliest memory is of putting a silver streak in it with a glittery removable spray paint, probably the precursor to the spray men use to hide a bald spot. I think I was ten. When I was older I put a large peroxide streak in my hair. My mother gave me a Toni home permanent every six months.

Once she kept me home from school to go to the beauty shop. The next day I told my young teacher that I had missed class to have my hair done. Her astonishment and disapproval of hair before education was as fascinating as it was surprising.

At twenty-one, when my own dark brown hair began to have gray streaks in it, I didn't do what some women do, that is, pull out those hairs. I went straight to the drugstore for a bottle of dark brown, gave the instructions a cursory glance, and poured it on. Those were the days of doing all sorts of weird things to your hair yourself. I recall my sister ironing her hair and wrapping it in frozen orange juice cans at night. Later I graduated to paying professionals to do weird things to my hair.

Will no one rid me of this hair?

I was married and in graduate school, and I was in deep depression. What do you do when you're in a deep depression? You do the thing that will hurt you the most, the thing which done on a whim will haunt you for a long, long time, like getting pregnant or getting a really tight perm.

There was a beauty shop right around the corner from my house. I had never been tempted to enter, but on that day, I heard a voice say, "Inside . . . quickly before you have time to think." I stepped in and asked for a haircut and a perm. I saw quite clearly that at twenty-two, I was fifty years younger than any woman in the shop, but that didn't stop me.

The beautician said, "What luck. We can fit you in right now, before you come to your senses," or something like that and I smiled the wan smile of the courageous but stupid woman on her way to the guillotine to give her life for someone who has already escaped to Switzerland. One and a half hours later I came out of the shop looking like a poodle with a bad perm.

My husband and I had plans to see *Lawrence of Arabia* that night and the fact that I had done something hideous to my hair to spite him did nothing to change that. "Please put a scarf on your head," he asked, looking faint and furious. I did. We went.

The next day I visited another beauty shop to see if there was anything I could do about my hair. The stylist said, "If I had your perm, I would kill myself." But I didn't. I went on to become a humorist and I think I have the perm to thank for it.

Mary Ann's dangerous permanent

A dear friend with fine hair expressed the desire to get her hair permed. Now, I am a Chicagoan. And Chicagoans, like New Yorkers, always know the best way to get somewhere on public transportation and the answer to every question.

"Mary Ann," I said, touching her hair, "you have very fine hair which probably takes a curl very easily. I can recommend the brand Oh So Natural." (You can hardly expect me to give their actual name, exposing me to lawsuits, even though it might save you from the fate of my friend.) "They make a gentle perm for just your kind of hair. Ask that your hair be rolled on the large rollers, and that the perm solution be applied for the shortest possible time. The result will be a soft gentle wave, flattering and easy to manage."

Her hair fell out.

We were all influenced by the popular culture; our hairstyles often mirrored those of celebrities. I spent a portion of my childhood trying to look like Veronica Lake. When Veronica's hairstyle was pronounced dangerous to the war effort, she put her hair up, sapping her allure, ending her career. She skidded into alcoholism and ended up as a waitress in New York.

The girlfriends get permed

We're sitting around at Sally's, painting our toenails and waiting for the apocalypse when Bitsy says, "I can remember how my hair looked on every important day in American history. I can remember what my hair looked like the day that

Kennedy died, the day I read that Reagan had Alzheimer's." "Too easy," I say. "The day Kennedy died you were wearing your hair like Jackie and the day of Reagan's announcement you started wearing your hair like Nancy."

"I started wearing big hair in solidarity with Bill Clinton the first day of his almost impeachment," I added. "So did I," Sally added.

This is the test of my friendship with Sally. For all the years I have known her, Sally has worn a scarf wrapped around her head. None of us has actually seen her hair.

"Sally," I say, looking at my nails to lull her into a false sense of security, "can we see your hair?" "Well," she says, "it's not big anymore. So there's really no point in your seeing it, is there? Unless, of course, you're motivated by base curiosity."

"No, of course not," I say. "You have a right to your privacy. Has your husband ever seen your hair?" She glares. "Okay, okay, forget it." I pause for a moment. "You know what would be fun? If we gave each other perms. We could give each other tight old-lady perms, tight ones on itty-bitty rollers."

"And then?" Bitsy asked. "A triple suicide? We'd be so scary looking that you'd want to stay at home and write that novel you're always talking about, or I'd paint something that needs painting, like the crawl space," I said.

"If we were all scary looking we would be forced to stay at home and get a lot done, because it's one thing to say you're going to eschew all social engagements and outdoor activities to work on a long-delayed project and then drop that project as soon as you get invited to dinner. But it's another

175

to feel too ashamed to leave the house, which is foolproof for getting stuff done," I said.

"And besides, if you gave us all perms, you'd get to see my hair," Sally said. "I confess, that did play into my plans," I said, blushing. "Okay, I'm game," she said, "but I'll have to kill you after." "Whatever," I said, reaching for the rollers.

Chapter 14
Find Me an old guy with Rhythm

Getting into the swing

On Sunday night I was swing dancing. "Swing dancing?" you gasp. "Surely you're not doing Pilates and swing dancing too?" I can hardly believe it myself. My mother would be turning over in her grave had she not been opposed to strenuous movement of any kind.

The first time I went swing dancing at a bar I had to have a straight scotch. Now I am inured. I go completely sober, unaided. I drive and park around the corner from the bar. This evening I sit with my group. I have taken so many lessons that I have a group. We sit together, or as together as people can that have never asked each other a personal question. We have never delved into the issues that might divide us, like politics, which might make it impossible to dance with each other. It's more important to dance than to agree on what constitutes privacy in a democratic society. I try to forget the man in my class who I heard say, in a loud voice, that women who cut their hair short will never find a husband. I'm sure he has other opinions that I might find even more annoying, but I like dancing with him because he is small and compact. I dislike dancing with men who make a big deal of crouching down when they dance with me. I am not a little person! Whenever we see each other, we say, "Hi, how's it going?" in hearty voices. No discussion is expected; a conversation that might lead someone to say, "Bush is still president. What could be new?" And I would get glared at, and then I would have no one to practice my turns or skip-ups with.

After I've had one drink, I usually walk over to some strange, awkward-looking man and say, "You look like you'd like to dance." He is happy to. I don't yet have the courage to walk up to the exotic boy who looks like he is taking a breather from selling something sordid and illegal, and who dances effortlessly and imaginatively, like a dream, and ask him to dance with me. I haven't enough nerve to ask a stranger who has fabulous style in clothing and movement. So, I ask the awkward boy. He says, "Yes, but I'm afraid that I don't know how." He is not being modest. I twirl him and dance around him and we are both pleased that we did it, and that it's over without injury. I go back to my posse, and the two old men in the group each ask me to dance. I comply, but they are so hopeless. They move so slowly.

I remember I haven't paid the cover charge. I run up to the front where my swing-dance teacher is collecting the gate. I'm holding my twelve dollars straight up in the air and I say, "Find me an old man with rhythm!" The Russian bartender, who a few moments ago couldn't speak a word of English, laughs and says, "Is that what you're paying?" I wonder if he would have been interested if I had waved a larger bill around.

I go home after an hour and a half. Several people rouse themselves from their isolation to say, "What? Leaving so soon?" And I smile and wave and say, "Sorry, have to go blow something up," and I drive home.

Men who dance

I met Marissa last night for dinner; I wanted to pick her brain on the subject of men you meet while dancing. You remember her, she's the friend who was so moved when she witnessed an old couple renewing their vows in front of friends and family that she made her own vow on the spot to stop wasting her life having a good time and find someone posthaste to grow old with.

I remind her of that. She says: "Well, really I made that decision earlier. I just didn't act on it for a decade. I was driving down Clark Street, near the cemeteries . . ." "Oh," I say, "right across from Live Bait Theater, I know where that is." "And," she continues, "I saw an old couple going into the cemetery. They were very old, and he was holding her purse over his arm and I pulled over to the curb and cried and cried." Anyway, as soon as you can say, "Wave your magic wand," she finds Mr. Long-term. She's introduced to him when the good-time guy she's dating brings Carl along to meet a girlfriend of hers. Kismet! Carl was married for a long time. His wife died recently. He likes to be married . . . he needs to be married, wants to cherish someone. He moves in. He drives her to real-estate appointments in the evening. He drops her off and then goes to find parking. She phones him when it's time for the next appointment. She can fit in a zillion appointments each evening and will soon be rich enough to afford a castle in Spain.

We discuss dancing and how it is an addiction, an addiction affecting a small number of susceptible people, fewer than those addicted to other forms of mind-altering drugs.

No, really, it is an addiction. Once you start, you can't stop dancing. If you are one of the pod people who swing, you are a dancer and we all know who we are and we are but one beat away from the gutter.

I run into a young girl from my dancing class at a club and we embrace each other. She says, "None of my friends want to come dancing, they just don't get it." She looks down at her top, which is satin and black lace. "I'm dressed for bed," she says, sounding surprised. The young man near her perks up. She and I look into each other's eyes with the intensity of one alcoholic falling off the wagon meeting another in a bar they thought no one else knew about.

About the men I have met dancing: In order of age, the oldest is Bob and is called "Bad Bob" to distinguish him from another Bob who is nice and a smooth dancer. Bad Bob is very tall and very old and does not move well. He dances exclusively with girls in their twenties. He never dances with me. He's a very bad dancer. The men I know say, "Bob is relentless." They are referring to his propensity for dancing with very young girls. Rich buys Bob a drink once every evening. "He is the only one here older than I am," he says. "I want to give him a reason to live."

I muse, "Perhaps Bob, who was happily married for many years and always danced with his beloved wife, is being true to her memory by not dancing with women her age." Rich smiles at me, pats my hand, and says: "That's cute."

Recently I asked my dancing buddy Rich to keep me company outside while I looked for a taxi. I wanted to talk to him without an orchestra in the background. He has never been married, never even been close to being married. He thinks that he is ready to fall in love. "I have become softer with age."

The unspoken rule at the Green Dolphin is that a man may never refuse to dance with a woman. He doesn't ever have to ask her to dance, but he can't refuse. On the other hand women have that right. They don't have to explain themselves, they just say no. My dancing buddy Rich comes back from asking someone across the room to dance. He says: "She turned me down." "No!" I exclaim, feigning surprise and disbelief. "How could she?" "She saw me dance," he says.

I met Rich at beginning swing class. Rich was not allowed to move on to intermediate swing because of his problem. I've been dancing with him at clubs ever since. His eyes light up when he sees me. He says: "Hiya, darlin'," and kisses my cheek. We chat briefly when the band takes a break. I have come to know and like him. I tell him my favorite line from a movie. In *Excess Baggage,* Alicia Silverstone asks Benicio Del Toro why he doesn't have a girlfriend. He replies: "Because I can see the end in the beginning." Rich is heartbroken that he never thought of that line. After a moment he decides he has. It's his line. Good. More importantly I have found a way of dancing with this man who is unable to move his feet. I say: "These frozen feet, it's neurotic, right?" He says, "Yeah, must be."

Once I thought it was my mission to get him to move his feet, but he is adamant about not moving them. So I have developed a way to dance with him and his condition. We do the basic swing step together and then he spins me out and I do a quick little freestyle riff and he reels me back in, having remained rooted firmly in place. He is a good person. Marissa says that she dated many men she met in her dancing days and realized that she hadn't the faintest idea what they were really like until they went out on a date and had an uninterrupted conversation. She's had many a disappointing date with men whose real politics were to the right of Rush Limbaugh or whose conversational skills were little better than Scooby-Doo's.

Now she has found a man to grow old with. She doesn't dance anymore, but I bet if I could get her out to a club and out on the floor again, she'd be a goner. You can stop eating chocolate, but just one Heath bar or coming across the word *chocolate* in a novel can get you hooked again.

Marissa and I try to figure out what is weird about men who dance. All right, women who dance. Maybe it's that we want intimacy without commitment that lasts any longer than the length of a song. Some swing tunes are fairly long, but that's as much as we can handle.

Chapter 15
When science is not the Answer

Bad news about HRT

The girlfriends are weeping. They have just heard that HRT—hormone replacement therapy—can increase the risk of breast cancer and doesn't protect against the possibilities of stroke. We are devastated.

"What's left?" they cry. Sally believes that exercise and a diet of chili cheese fries and free-range chicken will take her through this difficult time. Bitsy is betting on reading non-fiction, which she feels will put her right to sleep. She's starting with cookbooks.

"I'm going natural," I say, heading for the local health food store, which I usually avoid for aesthetic reasons. If they made it look more like a spa, I'd have more faith in their results. In fact, if they could just make it smell like a beauty shop, I'm sure they could increase their customer base.

Before visiting the health food store, I go to the bank and take out a home equity loan. Then, fortified with sufficient cash, I enter the store, in a spirit of reverence and suspension of disbelief, to pick up herbs to cure what ails me.

I got some ginkgo biloba, echinacea, St. John's wort, ginseng, walnut Bach flower essence, kudzu root, lady's slipper, licorice root, liferoot, passionflower, pomegranate, nettles, black cohosh, chasteberry, dates, dong quai, elder, false unicorn root, fennel, fenugreek, flaxseed, Honduran sarsaparilla, and soy.

Then I boil them all up. I was going to make a tea or maybe a poultice . . . I couldn't remember. They smelled so bad my mind went blank. And then I thought, "What did my mother's friends do when faced with the dreaded 'change of life'?"

The spirit of my mother's dear friend Esther rose up before me. She smiled. I smiled, and poured us a drink.

Post-HRT menopausal solutions

I run into two women at a benefit. I say, "I know you're practically out the door, but could you tell me how you feel about aging?" One is in very early menopause. She has night sweats. She does sleep through them, so she's not driven nuts by insomnia, but she's embarrassed in front of her new husband when she wakes up in the morning and is dripping wet. I am reminded of the 1950s when some women would get up very early and put makeup on so that their husbands never saw them without "their face."

For menopausal remedies, she and the other woman use a little soy, a little nettle, a little this, a little that. The second woman had one week of symptoms and never again. She does admit to mood swings, which cause her to blame her husband for everything. This makes her smile. The difference in symptoms used to drive women apart. Before they knew about the enormous variety in severity of menopausal symptoms, some were disbelieving. They would accuse those who suffered terribly of being wimps for taking HRT. After all, we all had cramps with our periods and we just sucked it up. I say: "Tell me something good about getting older." She smiles and says, "Sex. I just married a man twelve years younger than I am and the sex is terrific." The other woman says her husband is sure she will marry a younger man when he dies. She asks him: "Don't you want me to be happy?"

It doesn't matter what your mother said . . . words can hurt

When I am queen of the world, the penalties for saying *old bitty, crone, dried-up old prune, senior moment, oldster, geezer, old geezer, old duffer, old-timer, duffer, golden-ager, dotard, doddering,* even *veteran* will be severe. *Doyenne* is acceptable.

Sally is tearing the newspaper up. Now she is stomping on it. "Sally," I say, handing her the automatic shredder. "What is the matter?" Turns out the newspaper article had confirmed what we always suspected. Words can hurt. Why do some older people become frail while others run marathons? People who don't believe the stereotypes of aging live healthier and longer lives than those who believe they have become old.

Doctors who test memory find that if they flash the words *decline, senile, confused,* before the test, the subjects do badly. If they are testing stamina and flash negative words, they walk slower. They do much better if the doctor says: "Memory doesn't seem to decline with age."

Positive hearing problems

Lots of older people seem to have lost their hearing. This isolates them. But it also frees them. I imagine a woman who has a positive hearing problem. I watch her as the man behind her grunts: "Lady, are you moving or what?" and instead, she hears: "Lady, you've got lovely hands. Have you ever considered modeling?" She looks around and says modestly: "I'm a very private person. But I'll think about it." And hands him her card.

Medical disappointments

I e-mailed my doctor about DHEA. I asked him if it would keep me young forever. He answered that regretfully it would not. It could possibly, maybe be the way to stay young forever, someday, but right now there weren't enough studies, not enough evidence to support the fountain-of-youth claim. But what the heck, take it anyway. That way it would already be in your system when the proof gets here.

Can you believe it? Disappointing Doctors, volume one of You Can't Be Too Careful, my planned twenty-volume series, subtitled Watch Out, There's a Crack in the Sidewalk . . . Oops, Too Late

I went to the ophthalmologist for my yearly eye exam and was told that my cataracts were growing nicely, but not yet ripe. There was no evidence of macular degeneration and my vision hadn't changed much at all. Would I like a prescription anyway? Sure, I said, and when I reached the desk, the cashier asked for $30. "Medicare doesn't pay for prescriptions," she said. I paid. It wasn't until I was in my car that I realized that no one had ever charged me for a prescription before and that I had been scammed. I was never quick that way. Someone would make a sexist remark and I would have to return twenty-four hours later with the perfect comeback. Usually the person couldn't remember the remark and I would have to relive the event. Believe me, it's not worth the trip. Also, don't ever sue anyone. Lawyers are sure to be involved and they say mean things about you as if you weren't sitting right across the table from them.

I wrote the doctor a letter telling him that I was planning to contest this charge and I was very disappointed in him. His office manager called and rescinded the charge.

I started wearing the glasses. I developed a terrific pain in my right eye. Either a brain tumor or eyestrain. I took the glasses to my optical shop. The upshot was that the prescription was incorrect for my level of astigmatism and I had been straining my right eye to compensate. Another letter is obviously called for, but I just don't have it in me.

Could you write the letter for me? I'll do something for you in return. No, better yet. I could offer my letter-writing services. Writing well-phrased, rational-sounding letters of complaint is my métier. I'm sure I could do it for other people . . . as long as I was paid handsomely for it. Writing my own letter of complaint is too much like work. It's like the shoemaker's kids wearing shoes with holes in them, if you get my drift.

Unwelcome developments in middle age

A friend complains that she has recently started ejaculating during sex. She Googled *female ejaculation*. There's a gland. Usually dormant. She is incensed. "I am sixty-five," she says. "I didn't need to have that gland activated. It's messy. I hate it."

I resist the temptation to tell her about my one hair on my chin, because it seems petty in comparison to female ejaculation. Once during a facial the aesthetician asked if I wanted that hair removed, like maybe I was emotionally attached to it. I resisted sarcasm. I have swallowed the desire to discuss my chin hair twice. This is dangerous. I feel an uncalled-for remark about facial hair coming on. I should stay at home today.

1-900-give cheney hot flashes

"Hi, sweet pea. I'm so glad you called—I've been so bored I've been reduced to watching infomercials about self-wringing mops and miracle skin creams . . . No, I'm not actually going to answer the phone, I'm not that bored, but it's fabulous to hear your voice. You're looking wonderful. Everybody comments on how great you look—you're actually glistening, sweetie. Is that moisture on your face?

"Remember how your mother always said men sweat, women glow? Sweetie you're glowing like a nuclear plant. Don't worry, hot flashes look good on you. I saw you at that movie the other day, you know the one with that sexy scene—was it Daniel Day-Lewis or Kevin Bacon or maybe

Michelle Pfeiffer—anyway you were flipping your sweater on and off so fast I got whiplash just being in the vicinity. I'm kidding. I'm sure no one noticed, except that guy behind you. I think you may have injured him, but he had the good manners to remain silent through his pain.

"I know you want to talk about the changes in your body, but face it, nobody cares. . . . It's like talking about your cat: people get that glazed look that makes you want to slap them, but I'm charging by the minute, so feel free."

If you've been experiencing hot flashes:

Press 1 *and tell every last gruesome detail. Tell me about the first time it happened. Were you on public transportation? Did you think you had malaria but you couldn't remember going to Paraguay?*

Press 2 *if you have a strategy for handling your symptoms. Does it involve illegal substances and loud music? Are you taking herbal remedies? If I invented a line of heat-sensitive clothing that flapped around cooling you off, would you invest in it?*

Press 3 *if you've heard enough about natural solutions to menopause and would like good drugs sent to you immediately.*

*If your cat has hot flashes or is writing a novel or has an unusual hobby **press 4.***

Press 5 *to tell me if you are incredibly pissed off that nobody warned you at twenty-five about getting old, because if you had known, you would have devoted yourself to getting close to people who could appoint you to boards of corporations and you'd be earning big bucks for doing nothing at a time when you could really use the cash.*

Press 6 *if you think it would be great if Demi Moore could squeeze just one more egg out before the big M.*

Press 7 *if you'd like to tell me how you think this is the best time of your life. Oh, excuse me, I must have run out of tape. Thanks for calling. I feel so much better just knowing I could talk to you if I wanted to, you know, like if I wasn't so busy learning to drum.*

Think of your body as an old beloved car, perhaps a foreign car, one of those cute MGs that was always in the shop

I hate that Medicare has the authority to make me wait for two years to take a bone density test. I know that I have grown new bone. I want the applause from my doctor now! Not the nice one, the mean, well-dressed orthopedist who called me at home to tell me I had osteoporosis and minutes to live at that. I want her to tell me how amazed she is at my progress. Pilates and swing dancing have made me fit. Don't make me wait to tell her the good news.

There should be some provision for women who like to have mammograms, who like to have their breasts pressed like a panini, as long as you tell them it's a healthy breast. And I don't want to go downtown for stuff like this. I'd like to go next door for an internal exam, but no further. I'm sure plenty of women on my block feel the same way. If I could get a mammogram next door, I wouldn't even complain that every woman has to don that paper gown. Okay, I would complain, but I would mutter under my breath rather than go on and on.

Today my next-door neighbor popped into the café for a mocha and a special donut to go. Dennis asks: "Do you want whipped cream on the mocha?" Uh-huh, she does. We discuss doctors. Her doctor's office is right across the street from the coffee shop. I love that, but I know the doc can't be good if she's practicing in a little storefront on Roscoe. Libby says it doesn't matter what the problem is, Beth, that's the doctor's name, gives her antibiotics. They share the same politics, so they are on a first-name basis. . . . I tell her my doctor is very laid-back and his attitude is "Let's see if whatever it is cures itself."

I went to him when a rather scary red area appeared on the areola of my right nipple. He said, "Let's watch it." I had been watching it for what felt like too long already. So I went to my gynecologist, who's a bit more excitable. She said, "I have never seen anything like that before." She calls in another doctor. He apologizes for looking at my breast on such brief acquaintance and says he has no idea what it is. She sends me to an oncologist because it could be cancer presenting itself in an exterior form, but meanwhile she thinks it's herpes.

She thinks everything is herpes. She says everyone has herpes. Did your aunts ever kiss you when they had a cold sore? Then you've got herpes. I go to the oncologist. It doesn't look like cancer to him.

I go back to the gynecologist, who has the results of the biopsy: it's herpes. Well, if everything is herpes, one time she's got to be right.

I revisit my regular doctor. I say, "It's herpes." He says: "I thought it might be." I ask his opinion, should I tell a potential lover that I had an outbreak on my right nipple? He says: "No. It's like having a cold sore. You wouldn't tell someone you had a cold sore once, would you?" I lean close to him and ask: "What would Jesus do?" He starts laughing and motions me out the door. I have gone past my fifteen minutes of doctor time.

Daily expressions of gratitude: the tomato bisque of the soul

Thanks to senators Hillary Clinton and Patty Murray for keeping the pressure on the FDA and getting Plan B on the pharmacy shelves or under the pharmacy shelves or behind the dirty magazines. It doesn't matter that I am too old to have an unwanted pregnancy. I remember the fear. I am happy Plan B is available to others. I might buy a box just to keep them on hand for someone else's emergency.

Daily expressions of gratitude to those with money who have decided to do good: mashed potatoes with garlic and butter for the soul

Richard Branson, the owner of Virgin airlines and of many other successful businesses, has decided to donate several billion dollars to help the environment. This is good, but this is the same Virgin airlines that installed bright-red urinals shaped like women's open lips at the first-class lounge at JFK and expressed surprise that women were annoyed. They were sorry that some people were concerned, because they intended no offense. So I'm tickled pink that Rich is helping the environment, but a little gift to the women's movement wouldn't be amiss.

Memo to George Soros

Dear Mr. Soros:

In October, Dennis Hastert named you as the main mover behind the media flap making such a big deal about a few naughty text messages sent to congressional pages by Representative Tom Foley. He said that you were the big money behind the conspiracy to oust him and destroy the Republicans' chances in the November election. That gave me the idea to ask you to siphon off some of the cash you use to fund conspiracies against the Republicans to fund a few projects to help women and girls. Thanks in advance.

Chapter 16
Raking over the Past

I FEEL MY LIFE TOOK A WRONG TURN.

Yes. it WAS JUNE 3rd, 1987 At 3:15 WHEN YOU SEALED YOUR FATE.

The road not taken . . . was it a stairway to Heaven or a blind alley?

I have invited the girlfriends over. I'm using the good china. The meal is adequate, more than adequate because it's pizza from the good place. The girlfriends are rolling their eyes at me. They know I don't usually take the expensive route. It's a large pizza, double sauce, double cheese, with arugula and prosciutto, and wine with a real cork.

Afterwards I serve coffee with a choice of whole milk or 2% and next to each cup and saucer, I have placed a small pill. We settle down. Each of us has our own couch. My family had couches strategically placed every few feet, in case someone felt the need of lying flat out.

Bitsy sniffs the pill. "It's a half of a Xanax," she says. Audrey says: "You know I prefer Ambien." I bring one out.

"We're going to play a game I've invented," I say. "The perfect game for women our age. It's called 'What might have been.' We each have a chance to imagine what our lives would have been like had we taken a different path at a certain important juncture in our lives."

"Oh," says Audrey, "and the pill is because you're going to go first and take up the whole evening and it's better if we're relaxed and don't interrupt the arc of the story, but not so relaxed that we can't add intelligent commentary." Bitsy wants to know if I have any cake or presents to make the evening more enjoyable for others. I have, but it will be a surprise. "Can we pretend we're sitting around a campfire and toasting marshmallows?" Bitsy wants to know. I begin.

I've had the rare opportunity to see what might have happened if I had taken a different road . . . if I had married Joe (not his real name). I know some things. I know I would have lived in a small town. I know he goes to bed at 9:00, after a full day of biking up mountains, skiing up mountains, maybe ice-skating up mountains, and serving on committees. There's no movie theater in his town, but you can walk to the hospital and he likes cats. He has e-mailed me many photos of his life. I view them with fascination. I could have been his second wife, that woman ice-skating in a canyon, a canyon reached through narrow snow-covered treacherous trails, or I could have been his first wife, whose name is eerily like my own and who he chose over me because she was right there in nowhere Texas, and as he put it delicately, "You had sort of a dark personality."

I think if I had been his first wife, and I took a job as secretary in an oil company, I would have started drinking immediately and within a year I would have become an alcoholic and been shipped home to my parents. Actually, I think my mother and father would have come down themselves to put me on the plane in a gurney, my mother having a flair for the dramatic. She once appeared at the emergency entrance of my dormitory, holding a bottle of Robitussin and a tablespoon.

Then I think of the boys that really turned me on. The ones in clean white T-shirts, holding their package of unfiltered cigarettes in their rolled-up sleeves . . . while at the same time highlighting their gleaming biceps. Back when everything was seen in black-and-white and through rose-colored glasses all at the same time.

What if I had married one of those dangerous boys, those James Deans that I was so fond of . . . ? Many of us were such good girls that our only fun in life was through having sex with someone marked "trouble." What if I had married one of them? My mother would have allowed that only had I been far advanced in pregnancy. Okay, I get married. I wear white. I have a fight with my mother about it, but she insists . . . and she picks out the dress. She's utterly in disgrace, might as well get something out of it.

After our marriage I would have taken a job as a waitress in a diner. I'd wear a uniform and ugly white shoes with thick soles and my hair in a beehive, with several chewed-up pencils stuck in it, and I'd change my name to Ruby and everyone would confide in me. . . . They'd say, "Ruby, she's a good egg. She's had a hell of a life. . . ." And what of the mister? After a series of dead-end jobs he would finally find full employment in a steel mill, just a millisecond before those jobs became extinct . . . and every evening he would drink a six-pack of beer and fall asleep in front of the TV. Who could have imagined that his washboard stomach would now start under his chin? We would have lived in a trailer with the kids and a dog of many fathers called Lassie. My mother would have bought us a washer/dryer combination for Christmas and called me every day.

"Oh, please," Audrey moans. "What if you had started graduate school immediately after college and become an anthropologist and had a pillar fall on you in Egypt, and we didn't have to listen to this stuff as if we had never heard it before."

"It's my turn," says Bitsy cheerfully, and begins reciting the entire plot of *The Shining*, and then Audrey talks about how she could have had a future as a math genius, but she skipped an important exam to party and then we all fall asleep on our individual couches.

Advice for men

Today I came across an advice column for men. It admonished them to remember that women are raised to be good girls and that if they want to attract good girls who are longing to be bad, they should provide them with a little danger on a date. Make it seem as if they're dating a "bad boy." Make them feel they're breaking all the rules . . . practically running off the rails, taking the road of no return. Give them a taste of the thrills they might experience dating a young mafia don . . . without the consequences.

So if you're not a bad boy, perhaps just an accountant with a Harley, you can turn her on in a safe, yet slightly scary way by taking her on an over-the-speed-limit ride going the wrong way on a one-way street, or an evening of rock climbing when there's no moon at all, or settle in on the couch with a couple of joints to watch a grotesque teen horror movie.

If this valuable insight had only been available in the 1950s it would have saved me from dating a lot of unsavory characters, who turned out just to be looking for nice girls to redeem them. Bummer!

Reminiscing about the good old days

Normally I detest this kind of thing. How people were so honest that you could trust them over a deal made with a handshake, how it was so great when friends wandered over and suddenly there was a party and no one had to make ten phone calls, and how terrific you looked when you had thin arms . . . and no one had ever heard of underarm flesh that had a life of its own. My husband's pet name for me was "Toothpick Arms" in Hungarian. You know another thing I hate is when women say, "But I'm the same inside." Well, too bad, honey, toughen up.

Yet I do like getting together with the girlfriends and whining about how great things used to be before they became bad. Mostly we make stuff up because, personally, I don't remember them being that good.

Misleading events

When I was five, Richard and I lived in the same building. He was five as well. He adored me. I have a photograph of him looking worshipfully at me. I am beaming and looking straight into the camera. Several times a day, Richard would say, "Say it again, Nikki, say it again." Of course I thought it would always be that way.

In 1965 I got divorced in Juárez, Mexico. The only grounds for divorce in Massachusetts (where I lived) and in New York were adultery or physical cruelty. Everyone lied in court, said they saw Billy push his wife, commit adultery in the kitchen with Colonel Mustard. I went to a lawyer who had a room full of very poor people waiting to see him. He asked me to recount some of my husband's perversions. Oh, my! That was unexpected. I left quickly. I was reminded of the time I went to a porno theater with some friends from the office and the ticket taker laughed at us and said, "You won't last long," and she laughed again when we rushed out after seeing a man alone, in a raincoat, for God's sake, gyrate in his seat. Lying in court was not a road my husband wished to take. He took grounds for divorce seriously. He felt it would ruin his career to be accused of either adultery or cruelty.

He was not a citizen and so he couldn't go to Mexico. Wouldn't you know it? I had to do everything in that marriage, even the divorce. We had tried to go Mexico for a honeymoon. They refused us entrance. I didn't think they'd let him in to get divorced either. So I was elected. I was also the one who had to buy the cheaper winter coat because he needed the more elegant one for his career.

I was divorced alongside two New Yorkers. One was an attractive musician whiner and the other a plain whiner. Their wives had done them wrong and I was the first, but not the last, woman to hear about it in detail. They were not interested in my story of the two coats.

I went to El Paso the night before my divorce and took the room that was reserved for me. I was told to stay there until I received the call. It came. I ran downstairs and a fair-haired man in dark glasses gestured to me to follow him. I did. The two New Yorkers were bundled into the station wagon as well. No word of explanation or encouragement was given. No "It'll be over in one shake of a lamb's tail and you'll be good as new" was offered. We passed over the border and into a government building. The fair-haired man ran ahead of us and we hustled to keep up with him. What would happen if I lost sight of him? Anything could happen. Anything!

The New Yorkers and I got divorced together. I think to save time. No one in charge spoke to us; our guide led the way and gestured impatiently for us to follow. It was obviously a race against time, but why? Perhaps there were many other unhappy spouses from the East Coast, waiting in line to be free.

We were marched through a series of corridors and courtyards. I became increasingly paranoid, certain we were going to be murdered. After all, no one knew where we were, certainly not my mother. Anything could happen. They'll shoot us down in this courtyard, I thought, soldiers with rifles will be lowered down the scarred wall on ropes. They'll line us up against the adobe wall, nudging us into place with their big guns. I will be handed a blindfold and a last cigarette. It will be, "Ready. Aim. Fire. Splat! Splat!" And we'll fall like rag dolls. I have seen that scene in movies about the revolution many times.

At last we end up in front of a man behind a large flag-draped desk and we sit and sign and sign papers festooned with wax seals and red ribbons. The three of us are pronounced divorced. I suspect that I am not divorced, that the fancier the divorce papers, the less legal the document.

We left the room with our worthless pretty papers and the musician turned to me and said, "Will you have lunch with me?"

I thought, "Yes! This is how it will be. I am divorced and now the fun begins. Men who never noticed me before will be vying for my attention. I will date up a storm. I will dance all night, spread my wings, and do a thousand things I've never done before."

My elation turned out to be premature.

My friends asked that I bring back enchiladas for them. We ate them that evening. Otherwise, it was pretty much the same old thing.

My memoir, a.k.a., Everyone has one memoir in them, why not do it now?

I'm with the girlfriends. We're rubbing that new body moisturizer into our legs, the moisturizer that promises to create a healthy summer glow all year long. Audrey says to stop rubbing stuff on our legs because we are all too old to wear skirts and no one will ever see our legs again. Audrey has kind of a bleak outlook. "From now on," she says, "no skirts." As soon as she says that a slideshow of every skirt I've ever owned starts behind my eyes. I realize that I can remember every single skirt I've ever had, the color, the pattern, the style, and why I got rid of each one. This phenomenal feat of memory leads me to believe that it's time to write my memoirs.

"You're right," I said. "It's time to write my memoirs." My friends look puzzled. No one had mentioned memoirs.

"Your memoirs, really?" says Audrey. "Don't memoirs have to be chock-full of parties, drugs, shoplifting, sex with musicians, or at least . . . be interesting?"

"I have a sex story about a musician," I retorted. Sally leaned forward. "It doesn't count if he asked you to come to his apartment, but you didn't go because he didn't offer to pick you up," she said. "You know I hate to drive, and besides he sounded stoned and I was put off," I said. "So you didn't have sex with him because it was inconvenient and he seemed dangerous." She leaned back and folded her hands across her chest. "That's why you have no memoir."

"And," she added, "your drug experience is a nonstarter." I looked around. I knew I had told my one drug story to everyone in the group, but Audrey was getting so forgetful that I could probably get away with telling it again. I was about to launch the story when Audrey pipes up, "Is that the time you went to the Michael Jackson concert and everyone was standing on their chairs and you couldn't see a thing because your mother told you never to stand on a chair in a crowd and then Susan gave you a hash brownie and you hadn't had any lunch so you had two more, got stoned and hysterical and insisted you had to get out of there before the end of the concert when thirty thousand people would be leaving at the same time and you would go insane and have a breakdown and they took you home and you called me and kept me up all night because you were convinced your body parts were falling off?"

Leave it to Audrey; she can't remember what happened yesterday, but she can still ruin a story. "So what's left?" I asked. "Can someone help me out here?"

"Well, you had a father who was always in trouble, didn't you? He was drunken and abusive, right?" asked Sally. "Start there." "Thanks, Sally, but he wasn't sexually abusive. Actually," I said, "he didn't drink and he was verbally abusive. His favorite activity was reading and he preferred that to anything else."

"So let me understand this," Audrey said. "You're going to write a memoir about your father, even though he never beat you or won a Nobel Prize or even earned much of a living?" Audrey looks at me sadly. I had nothing. I don't care. I don't care what Audrey says. I can mine my memories of my father and work them into a best-selling book . . .

Alphabetically arranged memories of my father

APARTMENT IMPROVEMENTS: My father built kitchen cabinets and put them up in our rented apartment. When the landlord raised the rent, he ranted to us that he would tear out the entire kitchen. My sister blabbed to the landlord. I think she did it because she was proud of his wildness, which we all enjoyed except when it was directed our way. Because she blabbed, she was branded a blabber forever and she was never in on our secrets.

BOOKS: My father did not return library books. When the library called, my mother would take them in. One day the librarian told my mother that my father could never take another book out again. His library card would be confiscated. My mother wailed that he didn't play around or drink . . . he had to have something! The librarian relented and he continued to read at the table in solitary majesty. If my father had nothing to read he would read the back of the cereal box, the ingredients on the catsup bottle, matchbook covers . . . He read at the dinner table, in bed, and possibly while driving.

We, however, were not allowed to read at the table. I considered this abuse, but it isn't the kind that makes you cringe, is it? Because of my father's tyranny we had the shortest mealtimes of anyone I knew. We shoveled it in and raced off to find someplace to read in peace. My mother complained that we ate her dinners, especially her apple pie, too quickly, faster than the time it took to make it, and she refused to bake again. Well, perhaps if we had discussed current events at the table our meals would have proceeded at a more leisurely pace. Perhaps she should have chosen a more rational husband. Once she told me she decided to marry my father because she liked the way he smelled. Yuck, icky, too much info for a kid.

BUSINESS: My father started many business ventures. I remember the sandwich shop, which I liked, because I got to dance to the jukebox and bus the lunch counter. One day, in an excess of zeal, I removed a man's not-quite-empty plate, and he looked at me hard and said, "The last time a waitress took my plate away prematurely, I shot her." I felt honored. It was the first time I had been taken seriously by a grown-up.

There was a movie theater across the street from the restaurant and on Saturdays I was allowed to go alone. I promised that I would be back right after the first feature, because I was too scared to see *Kiss of Death* with Richard Widmark. I was almost too scared. I compromised with my fear. I sat in the aisle mesmerized by so much evil and that big toothy smile. I loved when he pushed the old lady and her wheelchair down the stairs.

My father started to worry and came looking for me. It's pleasant to be old enough to remember a time when a parent might just look for you, rather than put out an Amber Alert. Once my grandmother noticed that I talked constantly about a big dog I met when a babysitter was supposedly caring for me. Turns out the babysitter had another job and I was really being taken care of by three guys playing poker in a garage, with a big dog that they let me ride. That ended abruptly.

After the sandwich shop failed—my father's partners had a tendency to leave him before the doors were even open— he went into the construction business. He'd decided by then that he couldn't work for or with anyone else, people irritated him. On the other hand he couldn't focus on business details either. When the construction company began to go south, he stopped paying employment taxes. The government came after him. They garnisheed his wages. Before the federal government came after him, his clients and creditors were already after him. Just as it was my mother's responsibility to take my father's books back to the library, it was her job to take these calls. My father was reading twenty-four hours a day at this point. Sometimes she varied her response to these angry calls that always started: "Let me talk to the carpenter." One time I heard her say, "Jesus was a carpenter too."

I accepted a summons when I was about ten years old, after telling the process server that I didn't have a father, I was an orphan, and that I just happened to open the door at his house. The guy smiled at me and pressed the summons into my hand. My father had an exalted opinion of my abilities. He couldn't believe that I couldn't finesse the summons. He was furious. I had failed him.

COOLNESS: One day when my father and I were out for a

ride (we drove around a lot, everybody did) he got a speeding ticket. He tore the ticket up in front of the cop and let the pieces blow in the wind. That was pretty cool. Later that week the police came to visit; I met one of them as he was leaving the house and I was coming up the walk. The neighbors said he was just selling tickets to the policemen's ball. They wanted to protect me from the consequences of my father's bad behavior.

My father was also a cool dancer. He taught my sister and me to do the Lindy Hop, and even though she has absolutely no pleasant memories of him, she still does the Lindy, which makes us the only two women outside of assisted living to still do the Lindy. At his funeral, women stood up all over the room and said he was sexy and a great dancer. Which makes me wonder just how devoted he was to my mother. . . . My mother's best friend Olga once told me that he called her up and told her he was in love with her. She said, "No, you're not," and hung up on him.

SURPRISING SKILLS: I was wearing a navy blue jacket and matching skirt with a white blouse. As we were leaving the house, my father noticed that the cuffs on the blouse were too long and none too clean. We were all marched back to the house. While he ranted about my appearance he shortened the cuffs on my blouse and washed and ironed them. Only then could we proceed silently out the door, the day ruined before it started. On the other hand, only my father could have come up with the strategy of dressing me as a grown-up with lipstick and nylons, and smuggling me up the back stairs of the hospital to see my mother and my new sister.

UNEXPECTED UTTERANCES: I heard my father on the phone. The conversation seemed tense. Perhaps it was an angry client. Perhaps he hadn't shown up at the job for weeks. There was no shouting on his side, when he suddenly said in the calmest of voices, "You're an unmitigated prick, aren't you?" I would have recounted that story at his funeral if I hadn't still been angry with him.

Everybody said that I was just like my father, but I knew it wasn't enough to be pigheaded, people had to be intimidated by you. Once my father said to me, "We are the strong ones, we have to protect your mother and sister." I basked in the compliment, but I wanted to ask, "Who's going to protect me from you?" But I was too young.

My parents were a mystery to me. What kept those two together? At one time in my life I became obsessed with knowing what they were really like. I asked every friend of theirs who was still breathing to tell me what they were like. All of them said they were very nice. Only my mother's best friend Olga said, "Your father was kind of mean." She refused to go further. There were no letters, no revealing journals. My mother kept one of my ballet slippers, one of my sister's baby shoes, and all of my fathers LPs without the album covers. Maybe that's why I always wanted to be a detective.

Once my cousin Phil brought a tape recorder to a family party. We asked the old ones to tell stories. They told the same ones we had heard so often before. They were caught in a rut. My mother brought out the dog-eared story about the time she separated briefly from my father and had an affair. She said she realized she had a better sexual partner at home and went back to my father. . . . Tell me another one.

My mother returned to my father because he broke his leg skiing and friends pressured her, and most importantly, as a single woman, she would have had to live with my grandmother, so she chose him.

I had no idea how to get them to open up further. I got in touch with Marilyn, who had lived above us on the third floor. Her parents were adamant that even though she was a schoolteacher, and over twenty-one, she was not to live alone. She would leave their home only when she married. They gave her the bedroom in their one-room apartment and they slept on the couch in the dining room. I also slept on the couch in the dining room, but I was a kid.

Everything matched in Marilyn's room. I was awed. Her full-length shantung drapes matched her made-to-order shantung bedspread. When mother and daughter got ready for an event they would shower, put on their undergarments and then a robe, and then they would make up their faces. Once my mother voiced her concern that they would make themselves late sticking to this routine, but they reassured her, "It's all right, Shirl, we're all dressed underneath." At my house we had no robes and so were never all dressed underneath.

But carefully watched as Marilyn was, she managed to be photographed in the nude by a boyfriend and he, with great regret I'm sure, blackmailed her. I strained to hear as she poured out her heart to my parents in the kitchen. As I said, I slept in the dining room, and the kitchen door was closed for the conference. Certain crucial details were muffled. Did my father find the guy and beat the photos out of him? He was of that generation.

He wouldn't drive anyone anywhere, but certainly he could be counted on to be violent when required.

Surely Marilyn would have wonderful tales to tell of my parents and the glue that kept them together . . . the friends that surrounded them so that the glacial divide between them was less noticeable?

It was about this time that my grown cousin, Clare, moved in with us.

She came from Kenosha, Wisconsin, to work in the big city, painting the pottery figures that went with those stunted trees in glazed pots. She was allowed to come to Chicago only if she lived with us. She slept in the living room. I was in the dining room and I think my sister was in the bedroom with my parents.

I took Marilyn to lunch and grilled her. She said, "Your parents were very nice." I tried to interrogate Clare, but she had inexplicably become old, too old to take the train to the city. And I am for some reason unable to drive to the western suburbs, so that was a dead end.

I ask my sister, who is eleven years younger than I am, what my father read. I find I can only remember the books he bought me. I had *Black Beauty* and *The Bobbsey Twins* in hardcover. I had a complete set of The Book of Knowledge. He bought me a book of Bible stories even though he was an atheist. Did you know that people would rather have a homosexual for president than an atheist? I remember us reading it together. I loved the stories, but I knew they weren't true. I loved the song "Shadrach"; in it God saved the brothers Shadrach, Meshach, and Abednego from a fiery furnace and it had a compelling beat. I remember that at my father's funeral, a friend read his favorite poem:

It's about Abou Ben Adhem, who wakes one night to find an angel in his room. She's entering the names of those who love the Lord. Abou says: "Write me as one who loves his fellow man." She complies. The next night she returns with a list of the names the Lord blessed . . . "and, lo Ben Adhem's name led all the rest!"

Atheists like to have it both ways. My father got religion in middle age. He announced it. A friend asked me what form this conversion took, did he do anything differently, and did he attend services or observe the Sabbath? Or renounce atheism? I realized my father had announced his conversion and that was enough for him.

When he died I got his *Joys of Yiddish* by Leo Rosten. I always imagined it was a big book of Jewish jokes, but in fact it's a dictionary of Yiddish words with jokes as clarification. The definition of *chutzpah* is followed by this joke: A young man who is on trial for murdering his parents throws himself on the mercy of the court . . . because he is an orphan. Chutzpah.

My sister says my father's reading ruined her childhood and that's why she didn't read anything for a long time and why she married three times. Was she looking for a man who didn't read?

She says Dad read the paper every evening. She remembers that he read a book about Kennedy's first hundred days in office and that he and my mother took a business law course and that textbook was around forever. Mostly what she remembers is that no matter how cute or funny she was, my father ignored her in favor of reading. She said his obsession came in handy at school. He knew everything. He was totally reliable on obscure pieces of information and a good speller.

Every memoir I've read has a section on lost loves

A few years ago I read about a detective who reunited old sweethearts. They seemed easy to find. Possibly they stayed in the town they went to high school in or at least their parents were in the phone book. With all the new technology at our fingertips, why is it so hard to find my lost love? I'm looking for the last lost one, the one who was so handsome, so silent, so exotic . . . whose pleasure in sex came from watching my passion.

He was on the way down when I met him, but he had a glamorous past. He once lived in Mexico, stealing ancient artifacts and selling them through a gallery in Texas. He bought a ranch in Mexico, he had horses, and he had dozens of handmade boots. He got caught. He fled. All that remained of his past were two pairs of beautiful boots and the condition that caused him to travel with a roll of toilet paper in the back of his unglamorous gray station wagon.

The last time I heard from him was in 1961. He called to say that he was getting married to a wealthy woman and would be passing through New Jersey on his way to bliss . . . could he come and see me? He asked if my hair was still long. I was married. It seemed more trouble than it was worth to see him. Bill hardly spoke, I was socially inept, and my husband was a wild card. I couldn't imagine that our meeting would be filled with agreeable conversation and no long, embarrassing silences. I discouraged him. He didn't visit. I regret it.

I asked a friend to find him. A private investigator whose job was to search out errant husbands for the state and make them pay. He said he would do it. He said he was all over it . . . like white on rice. He asked me many factual questions that I couldn't answer. He hasn't called back. I guess he needs tangible information. I know he doesn't have a foldout couch or the soul of a loner. Is he really equipped to find my lost love?

I was twenty when I met Bill and not all that interested in other people. Although my mother had advised me to ask men lots of questions, to focus on them, I didn't. I am cursed with a short attention span. I learned virtually nothing about Bill. Where did he get his medical degree? He seemed old and sophisticated. How old? Would he be 105 now? When did he leave China? Why? Did he leave alone? Who was the American professor who took him under his wing, put him through school, and why? What medical school did he attend? He cooked stir-fry dinners with steak, and scotch in place of wine. He was kind. This is not the type of information that helps to find a man with a name so many others share. I Google him and there are too many Dr. William Chus all over the country. With his drug habit I could scarcely expect him to be the Dr. William Chu who became famous working on stem cell research.

On my sister's recommendation, I call a detective in New York who does background checks. He passed me on to someone else; the someone else had a family medical problem. . . . He'll get back to me. Meanwhile Bill is getting older.

Bill Chu, where are you?

Now I have found the detachment that comes when a love affair has been over for about fifty years. I think about how delicately he disappeared from my life. I was about to be married. He accepted that.

I remember now that I cheated on my fiancé with him. All these years I've thought of myself as such an uptight moral little girl, and there I was unfaithful, lying with aplomb. I think I remained faithful during my marriage because I was depressed, too tired to make an effort, but I told myself it was because I was an irredeemably good girl.

This kind of weather always makes me sad. It's a particularly beautiful autumn in Chicago. So beautiful that my eyes fill with tears for no reason and I find myself grateful and mystified that Bill let me go without a word . . . so gracefully that I never even noticed. I was, of course, occupied trying to find a Jewish justice of the peace to marry me. Bill left quietly and only reappeared when I was married. He made that one telephone call to let me know that he still thought of me. The perfect lover.

Hello, I must be going

Each girlfriend will relate her idea of the perfect afterlife, the one she deserves. How did we get on this topic? Last thing I remember we were talking about shoes. I must have missed the segue. I went into the kitchen looking for an after-dinner snack. When I came back the subject was death.

Bitsy says, "I hope I die in my sleep, that's the best, right? If not, then I want to be surrounded by you guys. You'll rock me and tunefully sing me into the Promised Land. Miraculously you'll all have better voices than you do now and some of you will not be tone deaf." "Don't look at me when you say that," I snarl.

"But what if it ends quite differently? What if in spite of paying into our retirement plans faithfully, we're poor and powerless at the end? What if my last years are spent in a hideous nursing home presided over by that dread character in fiction and movies: the large-breasted female warden with tiny features placed like raisins in her Pillsbury Doughboy face? No humanity in her and no outside regulatory agency to mitigate the ugliness of my situation."

"Perhaps I'll be eating grits in shapeless clothing in a raggedy frame house at the end of a lonely country road with nary a cell phone in sight. . . . Or in a low modern building off a busy highway, an institution, looking like some modest corporation pleasantly landscaped. No one will hear me scream or prevent the nurse's aides from putting my hair into pigtails and talking about me in the third person." Sally is already crying and insisting that she will never let that happen to Bitsy. I am not so sure. Bitsy can be quite irritating.

Sally says she knows she will die in her sleep after a surprising and satisfying sexual encounter with a boy barely in his majority. "Wow, here I am ninety-seven and a half and I'm getting it on . . . oops!"

I am jumping up and down. "Or best of all, we don't die. We just wake up somewhere else, as someone else. In fact," I say, "let me tell my fantasy first, because I know who I want to wake up as and exactly where."

Bitsy says, "You always get to go first." I ignore her and begin.

I have two wishes. One is to wake up in a beautiful place where it is sunny and between 68 and 75 degrees all year round. And the second is to have lost all interest in men, even movie stars. Every night I concentrate on my two wishes. I smile as I turn out the light. I hope to wake up in an altered state.

This morning is different. A balmy breeze ruffles my hair, the air feels soft. Do I smell the ocean? Perhaps today is the day. I open my eyes. My bedroom is filled with light. I turn my head slowly.

Yes, it's just like the photograph in my Pablo Neruda book. There is the beach, the sea. I have been transported. I will get up soon and go to that austere wooden desk, so like a schoolboy's desk, but strangely lacking in paper and pen. I am evidently a neat poet. I will sit by the window and look at the waves and write poetry. Someone named Maria will bring my coffee in my big white cup. Later I will go for a walk wearing soft wide pants and clunky brown leather sandals.

I try to sit up. I can't sit up. I'm in my fantasy and somehow I am paralyzed. Well, that sucks. I try wiggling my toes. They are in working order. Good. Not too serious. My neck is not broken.

I wiggle my fingers for good measure. Wow, I've got really big fingers. That's the danger of having two simple wishes. Others have filled in the details without consulting me.

I look down. I am wearing bright yellow men's pajamas, miles and miles of bright yellow pajamas. No wonder I cannot rise. No wonder I no longer desire men . . . or women for that matter. I am not Pablo Neruda. I am Nero Wolfe.

Okay, I can adjust. It could have been worse. I could have been transformed into Lew Archer, and no one would have brought my breakfast. I would be forced to use yesterday's coffee grounds scavenged from the trash. I would be sleeping in my underwear in my office on the broken-down couch that opens into a bed.

"Oh, my God," screams Bitsy, "somebody make her stop! This is like her story of her divorce in Mexico, the one she tells the same way every time, no matter how we beg. I will be too old for Heaven when she gets through. I'll probably have Alzheimer's by then. I'll forget my hopes, my dreams, my favorite food. In fact, it would be better if I had Alzheimer's right now. It's the only way I'll be able to get through this story."

I consider spiking Bitsy's coffee with tranquilizers. I want her calm, or even comatose. I don't care. "Look," I say, "if you let me finish, I will listen to you visualize the next world with perfect attentiveness." "You mean you won't swing your leg, go to the kitchen and stand in front of the refrigerator, and then go to the bathroom and then take a little nap and then start the whole thing over again?" she asks pleasantly. "No, really, I swear I will be your perfect dream listener," I say. "Alright, I'm giving you five minutes." She looks pointedly at her watch. "Can I start from the beginning?" I ask. The girlfriends scream "No!" in unison and pelt me with tiny pieces of fruit. "Okay, okay, I'll start where I left off."

I'll ring for Archie. If I know him, he's been up for hours, had his breakfast in the kitchen with Fritz. He'll bring my tray and we'll discuss my latest case or my lack thereof . . . my disinterest in the more mundane aspects of lifelike solvency is known worldwide. Let's be plain, my hatred of work is known worldwide.

I know that my breakfast will be superb, loaded with cholesterol and saturated fat. Perhaps I'll have sausages, made by Fritz. Fritz and I probably argued about these sausages just last week: should we use thyme from the former Yugoslavia, should the lamb be unborn, is the recipe perhaps too heavy on the basil?

I hope Black Forest ham is not on the menu. I have just seen *Babe* for the fourth time. I will try and nudge Fritz's genius toward vegetarian cuisine. But, as I recall, he is Swiss and they are stubborn. He may not wish to change the habits of a lifetime. Perhaps it will be necessary that he take a bullet for me, meet his gallant end ushering a client into the library. . . . The anorexic socialite daughter of the neurotic inventor who turns out to be a bit more unstable than we anticipated. Then I will hire a new cook, one who is not so dependent on rosemary and the flesh of animals.

When Archie delivers my breakfast he will bring up the dismal state of our finances. It's my cross to bear to earn the money to support my lavish lifestyle and extensive staff by pursing my lips in and out. I tax my brain to afford Archie's infallible memory and Fritz in the kitchen and Theodore up in the greenhouse.

If I had more money, I could add more staff. I suddenly feel the need for a masseuse. He would be called Carl and he would be from a tiny spot on the map outside Munich. I think as long as I don't bring a woman into the house it's okay to bring any number of new people onboard.

How will I afford yet another person, you wonder, with my great reluctance to do any work at all? Archie has a camera does he not? Perhaps I could take on a little divorce work.

There's Archie now. He knocks and enters with my breakfast. He looks confused. Perhaps he realizes he is not in Manhattan any longer. Probably wondering where the car is. He sets the tray down on the little table. He jiggles his leg.

I suggest that he call Lucy. I imagine she has a villa nearby, but before he goes I ask him to bring my globe up from the office.

Now he looks utterly dumbfounded. My request is unprecedented. I always play with my globe in the office. It's never moved. It's heavy, but he can handle it, and he'd better get used to moving stuff around. This is only the first of many changes.

I'm feeling tired. Well, I'm carrying a lot of weight

around. I want to stay in bed a little longer. I need time to get used to the new me. I must have my globe and my beer in bed. I will keep tabs on my beer intake by throwing the bottle caps under the bed, a surprise for the maid. Good grief. There's a void in the maid department. Who does clean up? Certainly not Fritz. Perhaps the new masseuse can be prevailed upon. "Are you still here?" I bark, and Archie practically runs out of the room.

This is good. I look at the book on my bedside table. Thomas Mann, *The Magic Mountain*. There will be no more Thomas Mann. I will pack Archie off to the library when he returns to get some Danielle Steel.

I adjust my pillows. I am happy at last.

I look around. My friends are asleep. Good. I begin again.

Sally wakes up and, without preamble, says, "When I die, I will go to Heaven."

"Of course," we say in chorus, because who is more of a goody-goody than Sally. "You have led a blameless life." "And I will be rewarded with a big, thick head of hair." "Will this favor be granted to other women in Heaven?" I ask. "Or will you be selfish and insist that everyone else have lanky, thin hair, greasy-looking hair, no matter how many times they wash it?" Bitsy asks.

"I will have thick hair and that's enough," she says. "You don't care what the climate is like or whether there is cable?" I ask. Sally is silent. "I guess not."

"Good, fine. I hope it works out for you." Bitsy opens what looks like an unabridged encyclopedia. "Now it's my turn." She begins reading the Bitsy version of what awaits us

at the end of that long tunnel. I am immediately bored . . .
then I realize that Bitsy is reading in French.

Sally and I look at each other. Surely what Bitsy is revealing of her vision of the afterlife is too personal to be related
in English, even to her two best friends. Bitsy is totally involved in her reading. Not wishing to invade her privacy even
though we don't understand a word she's saying, we leave
the room and go to a café.

Chapter 18
Born Again

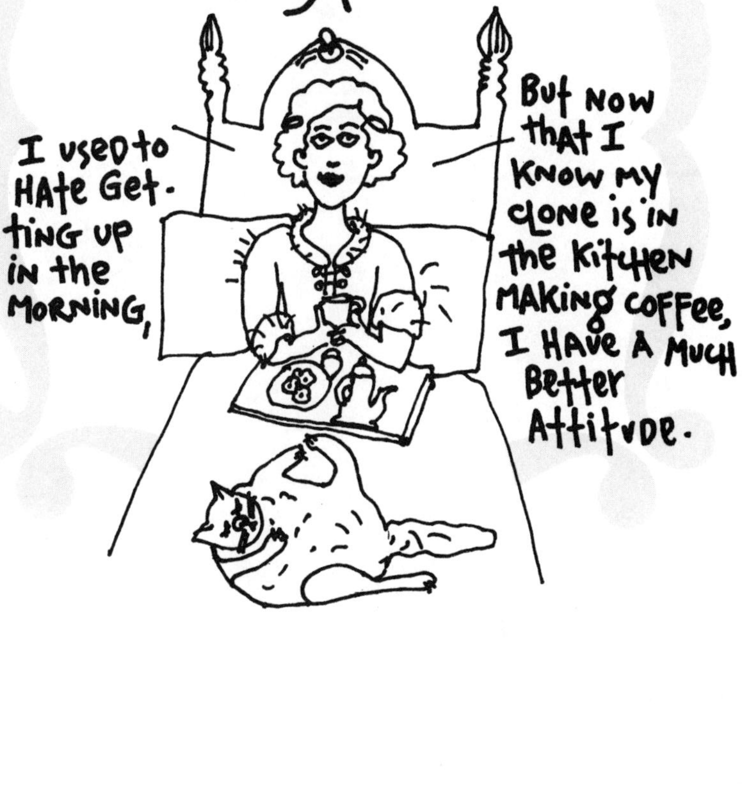

Finding a miracle every day: angels in dirty coveralls

The mechanic has my car ready. He's replaced the broken lights in my bumper. It's like my car has been born again with straight teeth. But still there is the difficulty with my ignition. Sometimes the car starts right up; sometimes it needs coaxing to start. It's not a problem of aging. Never tell me anything is due to aging. Tell me I need to drink more water, anything.

My mechanic has tried various remedies. He says, "Take the car home for a few weeks, see how it goes, meanwhile I will think of nothing but your problem. I will not eat or drink until we have beaten this thing. I will haunt eBay looking for the part that will make your car whole again . . . and put your money away, I don't want it."

Fooling folks into thinking you're younger than you are

Bitsy was excited. "Did you see that photograph of Jack La Lanne in the *Times*? He looked fabulous." "He must be a hundred and seven, right?" I asked. "He's eighty-eight and muscular," she said. "He says aging does not have to make you feeble—you can be strong and agile forever."

This gives me an idea for another career or at least a part-time moneymaking opportunity. I would teach older people to speak as if they were thirty years younger, so that at least one would get respect on the phone. In fact you could sound so young that you could answer classified ads for dates, arrange to meet someone and have the perverted pleasure of seeing them fall over themselves in confusion. "What's the point of that?" Bitsy wants to know. "You have to take your pleasures where you find them," I said.

One can certainly fake a lot in online interactions. We've all heard chilling stories of old men trawling for teenagers on the Internet . . . they are pretending to be a teenage boy, and perhaps she is a teenage girl or maybe an adult police officer in Vice, setting a trap for predators. Or the teenage girl could in reality be a forty-year-old woman looking for a teenage boy and in fact arranging a date with a creepy man her age . . . both of them doomed to disappointment, and possibly a prison term.

Before I reunited with my lost lover, he ingeniously supplied me with jpegs that chronicled his life from twenty-two to seventy. I sent him a photo of myself in first grade.

I was at my personal best at six years old, with a huge amount of dark brown hair, so full, my barrette could hardly contain it, wearing a white blouse and a short dark skirt held up by colorful suspenders. He was unprepared to see me, age sixty-five, stepping off the airport escalator. He looked stricken. Apparently he thought that I had remained the same while he had aged somewhat but still looked swell.

Men, more than women, tend to think they still look swell, no matter how old they are. I just read that men age better than women because they shave every day. The razor exfoliates and irritates, plumping up the skin, but I digress. He looked like a tree bent backward by hurricane-force winds or the sight of a woman who was not what he had imagined. He denies this . . . says he always stands that way . . . it's his bad knees.

I talked fast, using the voice of a young woman, one that I can train you to have for a nominal fee, guaranteed results, and he was charmed. I can also train you to have a young walk, bouncy and full of pep, but only on flat surfaces.

I've been reading about people who love the charm of old houses but are too impatient to renovate them. They don't want to hire a contractor to enlarge those poky rooms, put in new pipes, electricity, heating, you name it. They certainly don't want to paint it.

An expensive solution has risen to fill the need. The new house with rustic touches, as large as you want it, is available. You can have an authentic-looking old floor by taking a new floor and hiring someone to put waves and grooves in it, as if in the distant past children had ridden horseback in your Florida room. You can buy old pillars and relive your Southern slave-owner past even though your dad was a meek little accountant who ate the same lunch every day, made by your surly mother. This is all fine with me. It gives me hope. Why can't I have a brand-new exterior, with just a few quaint reminders of the past, like my brain, and . . . Well, I guess that's it. I'm not overly attached to anything else.

Important breakthroughs in digital manipulation: the eyes of a lemur with just one adjustment

Digital cameras now come with the ability to change the size of your eyes. The eyes are isolated, removed, made

235

larger, and then put back in place. An easy-to-use function for those of us too old to learn Photoshop.

Past life regressions

I'm with the girlfriends, eating appallingly expensive sushi, drizzled with a bittersweet chocolate sauce, when I realize that what I really crave is a past life regression. I pull out my cell phone and call my therapist, the one that specializes in treating past life neurosis.

"It is so rude to use your cell phone during dinner," Audrey hisses at me. "I'm sorry, but I need a past life regression quick. I need to know that I was somebody at one time, somewhere else." The girlfriends are fed up with me, this is the second past-life-regression emergency I've had this week. Audrey casually asks the waiter to bring out the dessert cart. The waiter reminds her that she is on probation, and she cannot come within five feet of the dessert cart, because last time she distracted him by telling him the kitchen was on fire and when he came back she had taken one bite from each petit four. Audrey is also not allowed to say "Catch you next time" or "Double or nothing" when the check comes. I'm sure Audrey had many interesting past lives that need treatment before she can become a fully realized being in this one.

"What do you think you were in a past life?" I ask Sally, who is polishing the silverware and adjusting the napkins into cunningly unrecognizable animals. "Never mind," I say kindly, knowing that whatever it was, it was irritating.

My cell phone rings, it's my past life therapist returning

my call. I explain this to the girlfriends again. Once you conquer your neuroses in a past life you are guaranteed a stress-free present one, where you will be energized and yet at peace at the same time, as if you were taking uppers and downers in perfect combination. "It's not as easy as it sounds," I say, "because you've got to decide which one of your past lives is exerting its negative influence on your present incarnation."

"Is past life psychotherapy more expensive than the regular kind?" Sally wonders. "We have a deal," I say. "I give her my barely used designer shoes in exchange for treatment." I know that I must have done at least one good thing in a previous life to warrant a therapist with the same shoe size as mine in this life. "Right now it's a toss-up as to whether my shoe and chocolate addictions are because I was Louis the Fourth's chocolatier in a previous life or Manolo Blahnik's great-great-grandfather."

"Perhaps you were Josephine's poodle," suggests Audrey. I excuse myself, my PLRT has a cancellation and I have to rush over to make the appointment, leaving Sally and Audrey with the check, again.

Dangerously stressed

You know how it is when you're obsessing about something . . . you see it everywhere. I look out the window and there among the cumulus clouds, I see the words: *dangerously stressed*. I reach for a magazine. It's not an escape, believe me, it's just another burden, disguised as a magazine.

I'm trying to read all these *New Yorker*s. Don't tell me

these magazines only come once a week, they must be slipping an extra issue in somewhere. Anyway, I'm trying to get through the pile and I read an article written by a guy who's forty-two years old. He just got married, he's at home in London . . . his bride is off interviewing someone in L.A. He has a rather bad headache at dinner, feels weak in the cab, totters upstairs, and with just enough strength to remove his clothes (this is an important detail), falls into bed.

When he awakens, his right side is completely paralyzed. Totally alone, totally incapacitated, he hears a noise and beside his bed someone, something in a hideous hockey mask, wields an axe and an unsettling giggle. He screams, but no sound comes out. . . . No, that's not really necessary. The reality is bad enough. . . . He's had a stroke.

The police have to break in and everyone has to see him lying on the floor naked, including his sister, but after all he is only forty-two and probably looks pretty good. (Whereas I am sixty-seven and am not at my personal best. So, it's lucky I never go to bed naked because, if there's an emergency, I want to be dressed. In addition, I wear a comfortable old pair of suede pumps in case I have to leave the building.)

He recovers from the stroke in increments. He's forced to slow down. A trip to the mailbox takes all his strength. He has to rest for hours afterward.

I think about taking to my bed. Many nineteenth-century daughters of the wealthy who did not have strokes took to their beds, leaving them only to write exquisite observations in their leather-bound journals at tiny painted desks or to make extended visits to the houses of old school chums.

But just deciding not to get up is no longer an option.

That's gone out of fashion. Someone in the family has to have a good income to support that kind of depression. If someone in the average family doesn't get up . . . after a few days you fill them full of a serotonin-based drug, get them back to work as soon as possible. An NEA grant for a performance piece on what one looks and smells like after having taken to their bed, done in real time, is also no longer an option.

So we are left with the catastrophic event as a way to change our lives, to find time to write in our journals, to find beauty in the smallest thing. I know complete physical collapse seems a drastic way off this treadmill, but I can't discount it.

Ain't no mountain high enough

In Chicago, old women are employed in the winter—you know how hard our winters are. They are employed to walk down the side streets of this harsh city whenever the temperature and the wind chill combine to go into double digits below zero.

You look out on a snowy morning, no, let's say it's too cold to snow, but the snow still lies upon the ground, no longer magical, sparkling and white, but hard-packed, gray and yellow in patches. And the sky has been dark for days, and as I have said, it's very cold.

It's 7:00 A.M. Barely light and you know you should begin your morning. You should be showering, getting ready for work, and instead you murmur to your cat, "Today I will not go to work. Today I will call in sick. Sick with that terrible flu with the symptoms that no one even wants to hear about . . . the puking one that hangs on forever. Today I will cough into the phone and say I am unwell. In fact, I will call in right now at seven oh three and not even have to speak to an individual. I will leave a message on voice mail."

I have my hand on the phone when I see her outside my window. She is wrapped in a shabby coat of indeterminate color, a woolen scarf tied around her head, with a cap pulled down over it.

These women always wear two hats. She is at least seventy, perhaps eighty-three, and she trudges along, pulling a shopping cart behind her. She has been to the Laundromat at dawn. I put down the phone and get dressed. She makes Chicago the city that works.

About the Author...

Gustav, the creative urge is upon me! Quickly bring pen, paper and some ripe CANDY CORN!

At once Milady! Will that be all?

About eight years ago I noticed that I was aging. That was a bit late to start noticing. A whole lot of denial was going on. At age forty, I had given birth to a cartoon character. I carried her full-term. She would do my aging for me. Sylvia would be my mentor . . . whacking at the difficult path ahead of me with her machete. She would always be ten years older than me. She would always have attitude.

As I noticed the signs of aging in myself, I found I was unable to visit them on Sylvia. So while as a smoker she should have a persistent hacking cough and ugly little lines around her mouth, her skin remains as fresh and unlined as on the day she was born. Sometimes she even got thinner while retaining her unlimited appetite for donuts. She was unchanged. I was her portrait of Dorian Gray.

As a student I was torn between choosing a career in which I would help others and one where I would stand in front of a canvas painting images from my darker self. I discussed my dilemma with a counselor at a Boston school for social workers. He said, "You have to choose, there's no good way to combine the two. You could use your talents as an art therapist, but I don't know if that's a good solution for you." I just needed someone to state it plainly. I decided. I didn't want to be an art therapist. What I didn't like about painting was the claustrophobic aspect. Just my depression, the canvas and me.

Before I found my calling as a cartoonist I had a great

many jobs. This was considered mandatory in my family. Our boredom threshold was so low. We perused the want ads looking, looking for that magical job masquerading under a mundane heading like: Clerk-typist, Army Corps of Engineers, must work with ditto masters and be untroubled by purple residue on clothing.

I worked in a bakery only one day, until they found out I wasn't sixteen, not long enough to learn to use the string machine to tie up cake boxes. I was an assistant in a day care center, cautioned to stop wearing bright scarves, as this excited the children. I taught perspective drawing without knowing perspective and hat making at the Park District. The Park District jobs were very well paid. You had to be politically connected. My grandmother worked during elections as a poll judge. That was enough, she was my clout. I took hat-making lessons, right before I went on to teach the course. It was a snap. Women wore little spring hats that looked like sanitary pads, and covered them with small flowers and a veil. The trick was not to sew the petals down too tightly, just tack them to keep that perky fresh look.

I went on to get an MFA, which gave me the credentials to work as a caseworker for the Cook County Department of Public Aid. (If you had a college degree and were breathing, you were offered a job.) Actually, even with their lax standards they weren't too keen on hiring me. They thought I might be too shy for the demands of working in the field. The waiting room was full of misfit artists and writers looking for employment. One of them I knew from art school . . . a serial killer waiting to happen.

Later, I got a job as a graphic designer, also because of my

MFA, and somehow developed the skills, even though left-handed, to do the job. Picture other designers scratching their heads and discussing which side of the board I should place the T square. I designed the cards that held that little metal calendar that independent insurance agents fastened to their watches; I got fired for going to a therapist. Their thinking was that since I had lied on the application I was unfit to be an employee. They admitted it was true that if I had said I was in therapy they would never have hired me. So lying wasn't really a bad decision. I worked there for a year and got my therapy paid for. My worst job was making cold calls for a bank—I can't even remember what they hoped I would accomplish or what product I was supposed to be selling. I hated bothering people. Most of them got rid of me quickly. This job didn't teach me compassion. I hang up without a word when I'm cold-called. When I was a student I had a job at the University Union Building serving frozen custards. We weren't supposed to eat them, so we would squeeze a little into a condiment cup and chug it down. This was my first experience with brain freeze. I also worked at a deli making Italian beef sandwiches. I was chided by the owner for using too much beef. "What! Are you related to these guys? You're killing me, why don't you just give it away?"

After I was fired from the insurance company I decided to become a freelancer. Even though the insurance company had fired me for lying, they were willing to hire me as an outside consultant. My future was sealed. I decided, just as my father before me, that I couldn't work for anyone, everyone irritated me, so I became a freelance designer. I redesigned a feminist publication and did my first cartoon in it. I designed photo buttons for a nutcase that I would confer with at Walgreen's because I was afraid to let him in my office. I have had my office locked up by the sheriff. I am chagrined to admit that it wasn't my bad checks that caused the lockout, but my office mates.

I've always worked for not-for-profit organizations. I begged a designer who stood up at an Artists' Guild meeting and argued brilliantly for unionizing our guild for a job. I was longing to be near a hero of the people, but he turned out to be an unpleasant self-centered jerk. Oh, well.

Only when I started working for the *Spokeswoman*, a national feminist newsletter, as a designer and illustrator did I see that I could combine drawing, humor, and politics and I was hooked. I was encouraged to draw as many piglike judges as my heart desired.

I found my career at forty. I became a syndicated cartoonist. That turned me into an optimist. I got my first cat. I fell madly in love at forty. Between forty and sixty, I must have been doing something, but I can't remember. At sixty I had a wonderful birthday party at an elegant restaurant in New York.

At sixty-two I bought a building with friends. It's like a marriage, with all the negotiations and compromises that I hoped to avoid by not being married. It's like *Big Love* without the sex. It's conveniently located near my coffee shop where I fall in and out of love every month and meet a lot of nice dogs who I am not walking. I have a favorite restaurant nearby, with good food and service so slow, I can write two jokes while waiting for my entrée, and the waiter knows I never eat bread and don't like ice cubes.

The three girlfriends in the book are more like six or seven. A bit of one friend, a bit of another, with the names changed to protect me from savage attacks at dinner and the scenarios made out of whole cloth. We are all pretty close in age. Suzy, my old college roommate, thank goodness, is a year older than I. We have all been together about 445 years.

I am the biggest fantasizer in the bunch, but not the biggest risk taker. We have all been married, some still, some with children and even grandchildren, though not gotten in the time-honored way.

We have had long hiatuses in our friendships. One memorable time, when I fell in love and became obsessed, I stopped returning phone calls. Suzy cut me off and I had to send her a postcard begging her to meet me in a bar, hoping she would forgive me. She did. The friend who ignored me in favor of raising her children, raised them and then we rediscovered each other.

Some of us have had high colonics. Some of us have made fun of high colonics. Some have had long affairs with alternative medicine (Ayurveda being a favorite), pyramid schemes, plastic surgery, hair transplants, bad knees, bad backs, and broken hearts.

My friends have engaged in exotic entrepreneurial experiments; one was led astray by fiction and came to believe that madams had marvelous conversations with their clients before the men engaged in sexual congress. She rented a studio apartment and hired a friend who had a matching call girl fantasy. It took her a month to realize that the men had no wish for conversation and were in fact confused by the opportunity. We ended up using the apartment for birthday parties until the building had a fire and we had to walk down many floors in the dark. My friend Tom urged all the women to leave first. I had only read about that in books. Moira was late for the party and tried to come upstairs even though there was fire equipment and water all over. She ignored the evidence. One of her finest qualities. One time we arranged to meet in a building that had a boiler explosion. She tried to keep our appointment that time, too.

When I decided to be a cartoonist I realized that I had no idea how to print the copy the way other cartoonists did, nor what kind of pen they used. My cartoons came out unreadable. I decided that I needed the help of a calligrapher. There was one in the yellow pages. He thought it would be delightful to write my cartoon, but he was too busy. He gave me the name of a calligraphy organization. I was given ten telephone numbers. No one answered their phone except Moira. I believe that's the last time she ever answered her phone. I found that it was unbearable for me to have someone else decide how my words would be placed on the page and besides, Moira had a cavalier attitude toward time. I irritated her with my demands. She said, "You can do this yourself and you will!" She fired me. Once when I was visiting she said, "There are some people here I'd like you to meet." I said, "I don't do social stuff. I can't imagine wanting to meet anyone." She said, "The handsomest man in Chicago is upstairs." I said, "Okay, what the hell," and he and I were together for a long time.

Some of us had our apartments burned down because of difficult family members, have written those family members out of our lives and back again; have changed jobs, professions, husbands, and addresses countless times. But our friendships remain. Oh, I know that was pretty sentimental for me. Don't worry; I'll never say it again.

Alternative titles

Questionable Strategies for Aging Gracefully

Confessions of an Irritable Woman

Tiny Whipped Cream Cakes Served Continuously:
A Strategy for Aging Gracefully

Women Up to No Good

Pass Me the Spike Heels, I'm Hitting the Road

Epiphanies in High Heels

Women Drinking Too Much Coffee

Don't Make Me Laugh: The Irritable Woman Gets Older

Don't Give Me Your Seat, Just Your Wallet

Second Helpings

I Didn't Forget . . . I Just Didn't Want To

Let Someone Else Age Gracefully

Swing Dancing on the Planet Denial

More Wine, Less Whining

Dressing in the Dark

Feet First: Strategies for Aging from the Planet Ferragamo

I'm Taking It with Me

Shopping Until the Very Last Minute

Putting Off Aging Until the Last Minute

Putting Off Aging: One Last Pair of Fabulous,
Uncomfortable Shoes

Dressing Inappropriately and Talking Loud in Public Places:
Strategies for Aging with Attitude

Crème Brûlée for the Soul

Acknowledgments

to Kris, my EDITOR

Thank you M.K. for bringing me to the 21st Annual Conference of the Journalism & Women Symposium and to the women of JAWS, who gave me the response we all dream of, and to Gail Ross who said, "I can sell your book"—and did.

ALL other EDitors
↓